LITTLE PRINCES

LITTLE PRINCES

FROM CRADLE TO CROWN

Sue Arnold

SIDGWICK & JACKSON
LONDON

For Chloe, Helen, Nellie and Tom.
And Catherine.

First published in Great Britain in 1982
by Sidgwick & Jackson Limited

ISBN 0-283-98598-4

Photoset by Robcroft Ltd, London WC1
Printed in Great Britain by Mansell (Bookbinders) Ltd,
Witham, Essex
for Sidgwick & Jackson Limited
1 Tavistock Chambers, Bloomsbury Way
London WC1A 2SG

Contents

I

A Delicate Condition

'It is announced by Buckingham Palace that the Princess of Wales is expecting a baby in June next year.'

The fateful nineteen words that mercifully put paid to the insistent and, at times, indecent speculation were issued from Buckingham Palace on the morning of Thursday, 5 November 1981. Ever since she and Prince Charles had returned from their Mediterranean honeymoon in September press and public alike had been agog as to the Princess's maternal condition – is she or isn't she, will she be by Christmas, by Easter, by her twenty-first birthday, by the Glorious Twelfth? When everyone had at last stopped counting nine months on their fingers, subtracting them from June, adding a couple of weeks for luck and then taking the answer away from 29 July, Royal Wedding Day, it was universally acknowledged that the Prince's duty had been done, the Princess's honour preserved and, better still, hard on the heels of royal wedding fever we were heading for an even greater treat – royal baby fever. Up and down the country knitting needles clicked. The first of thousands of pastel-coloured baby jackets, bonnets and bootees began to flood into the Palace. The announcement, in the usual terse language of the Palace press office, went on to say: 'The Princess hopes to continue to undertake some public engagements, but regrets any disappointment which may be caused by any curtailment of her planned programme.'

But, as one would expect of a blooming twenty-year-old (at

The Princess of Wales, having just announced her pregnancy, attending a lunch at the Guildhall on 5 November 1981

birth her father had described his third daughter as 'a superb physical specimen' and twenty years later that early promise had been maintained), the Princess carried her early pregnancy with aplomb. The first three months of pregnancy are traditionally the queasiest. How does the old adage go? Three months ropey, three months radiant, three months raddled. According to the finger count she was well into the ropey stage when the official announcement was made, but only the day before had dazzled onlookers when she appeared for her first State Opening of Parliament. She had sat, solemn and still, on the edge of her seat on the dais of the House of Lords Chamber, topped and tailed by a heavy tiara and a rather tight looking pair of white satin pumps, listening to her mother-in-law's speech outlining the Government's legislative programme for the forthcoming Parliamentary session. On 5 November, the day of the announcement, she and the Prince attended an official and lengthy luncheon at the Guildhall and later that day she accompanied him to the Royal Albert Hall for the annual Festival of Remembrance. The following morning the pair of them were again on duty at the Cenotaph for the wreath-laying ritual, and a couple of days later they travelled overnight to York for an early morning date at the National Railway Museum. She certainly did not look ropey – relaxed would have been a better description. After the museum inspection, they flew by helicopter to Chesterfield in Derbyshire where the Princess, as usual, charmed the birds off the trees and the shoppers out of Sainsbury's during an energetic walkabout.

'How're you feeling then, love?' asked a motherly-looking woman in the crowd when the Princess stopped for a chat.

'Pretty well, thank you,' returned the royal mother-to-be. 'I expect I shall suffer for it later.'

And throughout the weeks that led up to the traditional Royal Family Christmas at Windsor the Princess, whose popularity in the royal league tables is second only to the Queen Mother's, continued with a busy programme of public appearances. She wore a series of warm, shaggy, and conspicuously voluminous winter coats, her favourite being the one in seasonal red and green check which set the fashion for MacDonald tartan booming. She switched on the Christmas lights in Regent Street looking for all the world like the fairy at the top of the tree herself in velvet cloak and silver slippers. She attended umpteen carol services in umpteen draughty chapels, churches, and cathedrals. She laid foundation stones and planted commemorative trees. With her husband she visited civic halls and factories unconsciously upstaging him at every occasion for, just as all eyes follow the beautiful ballerina on stage rather than her doughty uplifting male partner, so the public instinctively focused on the tall, graceful figure of the Princess of Wales.

As for her maternity wardrobe, off-the-peg designers waited, pencils poised, for every new outfit designed by her favourite fashion teams, the Emanuels who made her wedding dress and Belville Sassoon who design many of her evening dresses, so that they might rush through cheap copies for the ready-to-wear market. If Ms Buckingham, as she is called in the Belville Sassoon order book, wore diaphanous emerald chiffon to go to a Royal Opera House Gala, so did a thousand other pregnant ladies the following week. Indeed, she had had her first maternity dress fitting long before 5 November. The month before, the Princess had flown down unexpectedly from Balmoral to London ostensibly to organize the removal of her wedding presents from Clarence House, where they were on public exhibition, to her home in Gloucestershire. In reality, she had paid a secret call on Mr George Pinker, the royal gynaecologist, who confirmed her own suspicions as to her delicate condition. Immediately afterwards she telephoned the Emanuels to alert them that outfits for the fuller figure were now required.

Traditionally royal announcements of the delicate condition have been tight-lipped and delicate themselves.

> 'Her Royal Highness the Princess Elizabeth Duchess of Edinburgh will undertake no public engagements after the end of June'

ran the announcement of 4 June 1948. But once the floodgates are officially opened the torrent of stork-embossed *schmaltz* invariably accompanying a royal birth is released: newspaper stories about schoolchildren in Lancashire working their tiny fingers to the bone to produce a patchwork counterpane for the new arrival; interviews with strangely articulate white-haired sages who can recall the birth of the baby's great-great-great-grandmother;

astrologers commissioned by women's magazines to cast the prince's, or princess's, horoscope. Haute couturiers are invited to design monogrammed layettes. Tea towels featuring the new royal family tree flood the market and distinguished historians explain why Ethelred or Agatha are the obvious choice of names for the expected infant.

By the end of the thirty-eighth week of the royal pregnancy editors rack their brains to think of new angles. When Princess Anne was expecting her first baby five years ago, one magazine ran a competition to design a new royal baby's potty, with tickets for the Horse of the Year Show as first prize. The winner produced a breathtakingly ugly receptacle, shaped like a saddle, which played 'Ride a Cock Horse' when in use.

While this surfeit of sentimentality may grate on some – for one the Honourable Member for West Fife, Mr Willie Hamilton, who dreams about tumbrils clattering down Constitution Hill – the razamatazz that royal children arouse in their first years is, and always has been, a part of the British way of life. It is only logical. As a nation we are obsessed with babies: baby stores flourish, magazines called *Mother* and *Nursery World* thrive, popular newspapers rarely pass up a tug-of-love baby drama or a picture of some television personality's bundle of joy. And as a nation we have the oldest and most interesting royal family in the world, and demonstrate our affection for them by an insatiable curiosity to know everything we can about their private lives. Royal biographies are the bread and butter of the lending libraries. Nothing is too trivial for the royal biographer to record, hence some of the banalities revealed in the famous Crawfie best-sellers. There was one occasion, recalls the governess from Dumfriesshire, a graduate of Edinburgh University to boot, when Lillibet (as the Queen was always known as a child) attached some red jingling reins to her mentor's back and 'rode' her round the garden of Royal Lodge Windsor, occasionally insisting that Miss Crawford paw the ground impatiently like her favourite Black Beauty before a gallop. Royal babies combine the two popular passions of Britain and if someone would come up with a way of including football in the mix, we would certainly recover the Empire.

But has it always been thus? Has the news of the imminent arrival of a royal prince or princess always brought joy to the combined bosom of the nation? Indeed not – a glance back into British history reveals a startling contrast in attitudes and customs over the centuries.

Let us begin at the beginning. The first step was to conceive your baby, and then assume the time-honoured radiance customarily (and questionably) attributed to the expectant mother. For many royal wives in earlier times the delicate matter of conception has proved difficult, if not actually impossible. Pregnancy is a curious business which we now know with the benefit of modern psychology has as much to do with the mental as the bodily state. The mental pressure on queens to produce heirs, and preferably lusty male heirs, was intense. There is no sadder example of this strain than Mary Tudor, who burnt bishops for breakfast with the best religious intentions, and who knew that without a Catholic heir England would revert to the cursed Protestantism introduced by her father, Henry VIII. Mary's mysterious pregnancy, which came to nought, is now generally agreed to have been what modern obstetricians call a 'phantom' pregnancy. This sad condition has all the appearance and symptoms of a normal pregnancy, morning sickness, craving for exotic foods, even a swelling of the stomach. There is, of course, the possibility that Bloody Mary was barren and even without the intolerable burden of her religious convictions and her double-crossing consort, Philip II of Spain, she would still have been childless. Infertility, the oldest curse of womankind, has been the object of folk medicine and superstition since the beginning of time. But, before embarking on some of the ghastly cures – medieval French midwives recommended a stew containing among other things boiled puppy – the proper Christian steps to procreation had first to be tried.

A wedding was always a good start but not essential. William I may be the Conqueror to us, but he was William the Bastard to his contemporaries, since his father, Duke Robert I of Normandy, never got round to marrying Herleve, the beautiful tanner's daughter of Falaise, and carelessly died of exhaustion on his way back from the Holy Land before setting the record straight. The parents of bastard babies were supposed to do penance involving

Royal marriage in the Middle Ages: the cementing of a political alliance. Edward II of England marrying Isabella of France in 1308

a deal of white sheets and wailing in the market place, but it was unlikely that Herleve had time for such niceties. At the time when most young mothers are teaching their children the alphabet, Herleve was fleeing hither and yon from one Normandy stronghold to the next protecting her infant son from bellicose barons who were disputing the little bastard's birthright and his claim to the dukedom. Henry VIII's second Queen, Anne Boleyn, and James II's first wife, Anne Hyde, were both pregnant when they took their marriage vows. As for royal bastards, the pages of history are littered with them.

12

But if a wedding there was, the first thing to get right was the date. There were a great many days in the medieval ecclesiastical calendar which were considered unsuitable and even dangerous for conjugal activity. Lent, Apostles' days, principal saints' days, most fast days and the twenty days preceding Christmas fell into the clerical closed season for sexual pleasure. This was hard, there were dozens of principal saints, and left scant room for matrimonial manoeuvre. Royal husbands were invariably feuding, laying siege or embarking on long penitential pilgrimages to the Holy Land. Fortunately no one took the matter too seriously, particularly as another school of thought, the medieval equivalent of the present *muesli* and cheesecloth brigade, advised that men should sow their own seeds as they would grain. That is, in the spring, which clashed with the No-Sex-Please-It's-Lent faction.

Since the majority of royal marriages up to the present century have been tactical and dynastic rather than affairs of the heart, with bride and groom little more than pawns in the hands of scheming statesmen, the principal purpose of the marriage was to produce an heir without delay, thus further cementing the union. No one expected Princess Anne, product of an era dedicated to free-booting liberalism, to start a family immediately after her marriage to the gallant Captain 'Foggy' Phillips, for modern princesses follow contemporary fashion and take the pill. No one expressed surprise or dissent that the Princess should continue her equestrian activities chasing after Olympic medals and eventing honours. The surprise would have been if she had hung up her stirrups and settled down at Gatcombe Park to knit tiny jodhpurs. Like most young women today, Princess Anne wants to retain her own identity.

For others it is a different story altogether. Her own mother, then Princess Elizabeth of Edinburgh, confided to a friend that it was her dearest wish to have her first baby before her first wedding anniversary, an ambition she narrowly achieved – and now Anne's sister-in-law will be emulating this feat. Doing one's duty as a princess has traditionally meant first and foremost getting with child; progresses, pageantry and opening new wings of hospitals came a very poor second.

It is hardly surprising that the public and the press also participate in the eager anticipation of a quick result within a few bare months of the royal nuptials. Princess Elizabeth told her former governess that she fully expected to read about her condition in the newspapers before she knew of it herself. The pressure did not slacken after Prince Charles's birth in November 1948, for when the young Duke and Duchess left for a second honeymoon the following year to stay at the Mediterranean home of the Mountbattens, international pressmen hungry for baby news dogged their tracks. They bribed the Mountbatten staff for inside information, hid in trees and paved the way for a new generation of scoop-hungry, foot-in-the-Palace reporters.

Publicity has always been an intrinsic part of royal occasions. Whether the Royal Family have a right to privacy in their curious role of the national family is a matter for debate but, compared to the attention focused on the private lives of royal families in former reigns, the present royals, for all their aversion to the press, have little to compain about. Set against the climate of seventeenth-century life, when the courts were knee-deep in scandalmongers like Samuel Pepys, honourable forerunner to the *News of the World* hacks, the Windsors are positively monastic. One explanation for the intense public interest in the most intimate aspects of the sovereign's affairs was that people had an altogether earthier attitude to sex. When Pepys, for instance, records in his diary the details of Catherine of Braganza's miscarriages and missed periods he is being malicious certainly, but not intentionally coarse. The court, with its vast reception rooms and corridors as wide as motorways, was a very public place. The French were even more explicit. When Marie Antoinette was brought to bed in the Palace of Versailles, the common people were allowed to stand at one end of the chamber, behind the officials, to witness the birth. An heir was public property after all. In most courts it was usual for the public to wander about unchallenged, hoping to catch a glimpse of the king or queen on their way to church or to an audience, and there was little security to prevent them from doing so.

The nearest we come now to such relaxed practices was the occasion recently when tourists waiting hopefully outside the railings of Buckingham Palace were surprised and touched to see the Queen Mother powdering her nose in the back of the royal car as she swept out of the Palace gates. But in the past, what we would consider an extraordinary prologue to a marriage, that of

Princess Elizabeth of Edinburgh, having announced that she would undertake no further public engagements because of her first pregnancy, attends the Derby with her husband, the Duke of Edinburgh, in June 1948

Frederick Prince of Wales and Princess Augusta of Saxe-Gotha on 27 April 1736, was apparently accepted as normal. The seventeen-year-old German Princess had been offered to the Prince who, at twenty-seven, was whining for a wife. He had already had a son, Master Fitzfrederick, by his mistress Anne Vane, both of whom had been sent packing. Augusta arrived in London two days before her wedding unable to speak a word of English but apparently well-pleased with her intended, who was a remarkably unremarkable young fellow. He is best-remembered for the famous epitaph,

> *Here lies poor Fred*
> *Who was alive and is dead*
> *There is no more to be said.*

The truly bizarre circumstances surrounding the birth of his first child we shall come to later. The wedding service over, the guests, not many of them, for Frederick in true Hanoverian tradition loathed and was loathed in return by his parents – George II and Queen Caroline – retired to supper at St James's Palace. The Prince said little and consumed an unreasonable amount of jelly for a man with serious work before him. At last he retired to the bridal suite. Led by the Queen (who was convinced, despite Fitzfrederick, that her son was impotent) and her ladies, Augusta was taken to an adjoining room. With due ceremony she was disrobed, her white wedding gown removed and a white silk nightgown trimmed with Brussels lace put on. Thence she was borne (she was a hefty lass) like the sacrificial lamb to the bridal bed where the Prince was already waiting. His nightcap, recalls an observer, was as high as a grenadier's cap and fell over one eye. Augusta was propped up beside him, the pillows were puffed, the coverlet smoothed and at a given signal a long procession of guests, courtiers and sundry officials trooped past the young pair offering congratulations and encouragement. The exhibition lasted the better part of an hour. The groom seemed nervous, Augusta not in the least concerned.

Another curious first night was that of 8 April 1795 following the wedding of George Prince of Wales, later the Prince Regent, to Princess Caroline of Brunswick. Purely to spite his father – the Hanoverian antipathy twixt father and son worsened with the passing of the years – he had chosen to marry the least eligible princess in Europe. Caroline was short, fat, and not overly clean in her person, her conversation, or her morals. Her reputation for nymphomania was such that every waking moment she was sleuthed by a chaperone, even around the dance floor in case she behaved improperly in the middle of a minuet. The Prince turned up at the Chapel Royal in St James's Palace for the ceremony the worse for drink. He forgot the order of service, stood up when everyone else was kneeling and had to be cautioned by the King, *sotto voce*, to pull himself together. When the Archbishop of Canterbury reached the point in the service about anyone knowing any just cause or lawful impediment to the union, there was a significant pause.

At the reception that followed, George continued to drink heavily, steeling himself for the forthcoming ordeal. How anyone with such refined tastes and aesthetic sensitivity as the future Prince Regent could have landed himself in so wretched and irrevocable a mess is hard to understand. Maybe Caroline, with her dumpy figure and flamboyant clothes, appealed to that side of his nature later to materialize in the onion domes of the Brighton Pavilion. Or maybe his desire to score off his father had overtaken rational behaviour.

The consummation of their marriage was less of a first-night than a-morning-after-the-night-before event. Instead of leaping with alacrity into the bridal bed, the Prince fell into a drunken stupor on the rug in front of the bedroom fire where he remained until first light. There is a strong chance that he slept with his wife on one occasion only, the morning of 9 April, for precisely nine months later his only daughter Charlotte was born.

Despite her uncouth ways, Caroline of Brunswick had one indisputable advantage where princesses (especially princesses of Wales) are concerned. She could conceive at the drop of a coronet and virtually to order. Had she and the Prince continued to live together as man and wife Caroline would probably have produced as substantial a family as her rabbit of a mother-in-law, Queen Charlotte, with her hutchful of fifteen. But the couple never shared a roof. Relations between them became increasingly strained, and George asked his father for permission to obtain a formal separation. George III, not yet mad but heading that way, refused. Caroline's behaviour became more and more excessive

James Gillray's cartoon of a tipsy Prince of Wales being presented with his 'immense' daughter, Princess Charlotte, born on 9 January 1796. Charles James Fox and Richard Brinsley Sheridan, Whig friends of the Prince of Wales, are shown kissing the baby's bottom

and the company she kept less and less desirable. Three days after she gave birth to an extremely large daughter – 'immense' was how the Prince described the child in a letter to the Queen – he broke off all further contact with his wife. Retiring to his Brighton residence he made a will in which he bequeathed all his earthly possessions to Maria Fitzherbert, 'who is my wife in the eyes of God and who is and ever will be such in mine . . . To her who is called Princess of Wales I leave one shilling'.

Fate has been hard on princesses. Caroline had the natural ability to procreate but was denied the opportunity. For many other royal ladies the reverse was true. Catherine of Braganza's marriage to Charles II, even with a nursery full of rollicking little heirs, would have been no bed of roses, bearing in mind the Merry Monarch's concupiscent bent and appetite for sexual variety. But to have nothing with which to counter his infidelity, no child of her own to flaunt before the dozen or so he had sired by his more permanent mistresses, Lucy Walter, Nell Gwynne, Catherine

18

Pegge, Louise de Kéroualle, Elizabeth Killigrew, Moll Davies, and Barbara Villiers, Countess of Castlemaine (who mothered five royal bastards) must have been hell. Since many of his illegitimate children were born before his marriage, the King's virility was never in question. Catherine it was who ran the gauntlet of court gossip, whispered malice, and the open derision of Lady Castlemaine.

After she had been married a full year the Queen (then aged twenty-four and long in the tooth for a bride at a time when child marriages still prevailed) went to various physicians of repute for advice. She might well have clanked about with a load of moonstones round her neck, her wrists and her ears, for moonstones were supposed to contain strange properties for producing fertility. From Saxon days it was common for brides to be given moonstones as wedding presents. She might also have tried some of the many fertility brews on the market both in patent-medicine form or made up from the produce of a palace knot garden.

One sixteenth-century writer, Andrew Roodes, advised no end of helpful homeopathic hints for successful reproduction. They appeared in his contemporary bestseller, *The Fyrst Boke of the Introduction of Knowledge.* In page after page Master Roodes gives pithy advice on how to conceive. In a word the secret is 'sawge' or sage administered in a variety of ways. You could crush sage and mix it with honey and a little wood-ash and rub it on the soles of the feet before going to bed. You could make a soothing brew of sage, mead, and cinnamon and drink it as a nightcap. Chewing sage at any time, said Master Roodes, would make a woman fertile, but if all else failed, a mustard and sage bath at full moon would not come amiss.

However Catherine of Braganza lived in the enlightened seventeenth century, and more scientific measures were proposed by the royal physicians. Her Royal Highness should make a progress to Tunbridge Wells and partake of the waters therein. The idea that a spa contained some miracle ingredient which would immediately promote fertility is obviously absurd, but in the same way as progressive medical practitioners today might recommend childless couples to smoke pot to relax themselves mentally and physically, so in the past a spell at one of the fashionable watering holes, Cheltenham or Leamington or best of

19

Catherine of Braganza, the Portuguese princess who married Charles II in May 1662, but failed to provide him with a legitimate heir

all Bath itself, was a favourite prescription for anything from arthritis to infertility.

There was nothing particularly medical about spas. They were built more as holiday resorts with promenades for gentle strolling, gazebos, pavilions, coffee-houses, and all manner of entertainment. If the waters failed, the visitor could fall back on one of the many small shrines strategically placed about the area. People would plan their visit from one year to the next and spas were regarded as excellent centres for matchmaking.

20

The most famous recorded visit to the healing waters was made by Queen Catherine's sister-in-law, Mary of Modena, James II's Queen. Twenty years after Catherine's visit to Tunbridge, Mary travelled to Bath in the hope of producing a Stuart heir. Mary had had eight pregnancies with nothing to show for them and it was becoming a matter of some urgency. If she did not produce a son, the succession would pass to her step-daughters, Mary and Anne, both of whom were Protestants. Mary of Modena was almost as enthusiastic a Catholic as her Tudor namesake, Bloody Mary. She had relinquished her convent career at the age of seventeen to marry James only after a letter from the Pope advised the frustrated young novice that she would better serve her Maker by returning England to the Roman faith than by shutting herself up behind convent walls. Even so the poor girl had cried for a week afterwards.

Mary arrived in Bath with a great following of attendants who took up all the available beds in the city, like the delegates of a party political conference. She was the biggest tourist attraction of the season. Shortly before ten in the morning she left the Pump Room and headed for the actual bathing enclosure with its elaborately decorated tiles and shiny brass. Spectators eager to see the royal dip crowded the galleries. The Queen, wearing a primrose-yellow gown of French satin, slowly descended the shallow steps into the bubbling waters, surrounded by the Ladies of the Bedchamber who, like it or not, were about to have their fertility boosted along with their mistress. As she hit the waters the voluminous folds of yellow satin floated up around her like a huge balloon concealing the contours of the royal torso. The spectators broke into a round of thunderous applause and in the nearby pavilion an Italian string orchestra played a patriotic anthem. Had it been nightfall there would doubtless have been a firework display.

It is worth mentioning that when the present Queen Mother came to the throne as consort to George VI there was discreet speculation as to whether she might not enlarge her family of two small daughters, the Princesses Elizabeth and Margaret Rose. Significantly Elizabeth was not named the official Heir Apparent for several years after her father became King. Clearly the Queen was hoping for a son. Why that hope faded we shall probably never know. But it is interesting to think that three hundred years ago our much-loved Queen Mother, with her ostrich-trimmed hats and pastel ballgowns, might also have taken the road to Bath.

Maybe the spa waters of Bath had contained the miracle ingredient, for nine months after visiting Bath Mary of Modena gave birth to James Francis Edward Stuart, the Old Pretender. While the Queen had been plunging, King James had been making a progress in the West, stopping at every available shrine to add the fuel of faith to his wife's burning desire for a child. Whether it was prayer or paddling that did the trick is debatable.

Nothing, however, had helped poor Catherine of Braganza. At first she did not even have the funds to get to Tunbridge as her doctors advised. Charles had shamelessly appropriated Catherine's dowry into the Privy Purse and the small part of it he had allowed her to keep was now spent. The Queen sent messages to her husband begging for money but she was first ignored and then refused. In desperation she made a formal petition to the Treasury for funds (it was in the public interest to have an heir and therefore a legitimate Exchequer expense) and was granted £2,000 for her trip to Kent. The money would have been better spent on warships for Catherine returned heavy-hearted and empty-bellied. Speculation surrounding her fertility, or lack of it, continued to reverberate around the English and European courts. Some time later the King's sister, Minette, wrote from France to ask if it were true that the Queen had missed two periods. Not in the least surprised or dismayed that such a delicate matter should be the subject for drawing-room conversation in Paris, Charles replied that it was true but that Catherine had had a miscarriage shortly afterwards. The Queen was to have one more miscarriage before eventually giving up the hopeless cause.

Two other Stuart Queens were also destined to be frustrated mothers. Mary, the better half of William of Orange, had a phantom pregnancy not long after her marriage. She was much influenced in her attitude to childbirth by the circumstances of her own husband's birth, for William had been delivered a few hours after his father had died. The birth-chamber had been draped with black and the midwives who attended his mother were dressed in mourning. Could this gloomy tale have had any influence on her imagined pregnancy? Her sister Anne must be the most tragic example of royal motherhood in a thousand years of English history. Though she appeared to have no trouble

Mary of Modena, the second wife of James, Duke of York, who ascended the throne as James II. Mary suffered several miscarriages, and was dispatched by her husband to Bath to try to ensure the Catholic Succession.

conceiving, she had the greatest difficulty lasting the course. Those children that she did manage to carry to term failed, apart from the Duke of Gloucester, to survive much beyond infancy. Prince William Henry, who was queerly deformed, died at the age of eleven.

Since no book purporting to deal with royal children could possibly be complete without some reference to the teeming progeny that emerged from this dull and desperate Princess, this seems as good an opportunity as any to deal with the matter. Over a period of sixteen years from 1684 to 1700 Anne had seventeen pregnancies which, for the record, fell thus.

1   A stillborn daughter
2   Princess Mary, who died aged two
3   Princess Anne Sophia, who died aged one year
4   A miscarriage
5   A miscarriage, male
6   A miscarriage
7   Prince William, Duke of Gloucester, who died aged eleven
8   Princess Mary, premature, who died two hours after birth
9   Prince George, who died minutes after birth
10 A miscarriage, female
11 A miscarriage
12 A miscarriage, female
13 A double miscarriage of a premature son and a much smaller sibling
14 A miscarriage
15 A miscarriage
16 A miscarriage, male
17 A miscarriage, male

It is a wretched and doleful obstetric saga but not, alas, unique at a time when so little was known about the physiognomy of pregnant women and the development of the foetus. The stillborn daughter who initiated the procession of doomed children was due, it was thought, to Anne falling from a horse at an advanced state of pregnancy. The royal passion for horses was quite often to bring tragic consequences. Two-year-old Mary's fatal illness,

24

Princess Anne with her one child who survived infancy, the ill-fated William, Duke of Gloucester, who died at the age of eleven

apart from vague reports of fits and fevers, was never satisfactorily diagnosed. Too bad the doctors did not discover the cause, for it was the same convulsions that carried off the next daughter, Anne Sophia. Both children were buried in Westminster Abbey, Mary in the vault containing the relics of Mary Queen of Scots, Anne in Henry vii's Chapel.

Ironically the divine power of faith healing or laying on of hands, which was supposed to fall naturally upon sovereigns along with the divine right to rule, was said to last only as far as the Stuarts. If Queen Anne did possess such a power she did not think it appropriate to use it upon her own family. Divinity notwithstanding, there was said to be an excellent antidote to miscarriage dating back to medieval times, the herb tansy. A weird but not unpleasant concoction was made from crushed tansy, rue, honey, and wild strawberries. Now was the time to change your moonstone jewellery which had special fertility significance and substitute eaglestones to prevent miscarriages and threatened abortions. Eaglestones and their magical powers dated back to the Romans and were mentioned by Cicero. They were large, hollow, dark brown stones with tiny loose chippings inside that rattled when shaken. They took their name from the belief that eagles carried them up to their mountain eyries and placed them in their nests among the eggs to safeguard them. Anne Boleyn wore an eaglestone charm about her neck, a present from Henry viii when she was carrying her first child. Edward iii's Queen Philippa wore a girdle studded with the stones; others wore them tied to the hems of their gowns or as clasps on cloaks. There was another superstition which reckoned that if a pregnant woman wore a white scarf about her neck, a symbol of the Virgin's robes, no harm would befall her or her child. A cavalier attitude to pregnancy was taken by yet another Stuart Princess, Elizabeth, sister of Charles i, who became Queen of Bohemia. Elizabeth had nine children but steadfastly refused to concede that she was pregnant until she was actually brought to bed. She made no concessions to her condition and continued to hunt well into her ninth month.

Lest the balance seem too much weighted on the unfortunate and unsuccessful aspects of royal pregnancies, we will leave the pitiful memories of cradles never filled and layettes never worn and consider the more positive side of royal pregnancies.

A cursory glance at the spreading branches of the family trees of the English royal houses will reveal that our queens and princesses have been, on the whole, pretty successful breeders. Until medicine achieved a more scientific basis around the turn of the seventeenth century, advice on ante-natal care was grounded largely in superstition and old wives' remedies handed down from mother to daughter. But apart from herbs and charms, there was much sound, straightforward advice to be had in those early days. Exercise was considered essential for a happy pregnancy – no lolling or idling. Peter de la Primadaye, physician to Henry III of France, advised the King that great-bellied women should beware of living too delicately or too sparingly, but should refrain from drunkenness, as should, continued the doctor meaningfully, their husbands also.

Pregnancy was a time for the mother to prepare herself emotionally as well as physically. Expectant mothers were advised to avoid bad smells and ugly sights like public executions, normally considered great entertainment for the whole family including the children. Tapestries and other wall adornments with pleasant rural scenes were especially chosen for birth-chambers to replace the usual battle paintings awash with blood. So the husbands indulged their wives at this time. Henry III redecorated several rooms for Eleanor of Provence when she was carrying their first-born and pushed the boat out by ordering glass for the windows of the nursery at Windsor Castle. When Jane Seymour became pregnant, Henry VIII sought to cheer her by having her apartments lavishly redecorated and new tapestries depicting Arcadian scenes were hung on the walls. Jane's bed was hung with crimson curtains trimmed with gold, and she lay propped on crimson velvet pillows. Henry was enthusiastic about beds, not simply getting into them but actually designing them. For his previous wife, Anne Boleyn, he had ordered a special bed from France where the best beds in the world were made. French frolic beds dating from the sixteenth century are splendid pieces of fantastical nonsense. Anne's bed arrived swathed in pale blue silk hangings, though pink would have been more appropriate.

In contrast to this lotus-eating lifestyle, many medieval queens were to be found trailing dispiritedly about after their pugnacious husbands, giving birth in whichever castle (if they were lucky) or cottage (if they were not) that chanced to be nearest to the battlefield. Edward IV's queen, Elizabeth Woodville, was literally 'in the straw' on one of her husband's northern campaigns, giving birth in frugal conditions in a West Riding village. Similar peripatetic preparations for motherhood were undertaken by Eleanor of Aquitaine, consort of Henry II, who was constantly on the move between England and France, but even this was small beer compared to the alarming ante-natal activities of Isabella of Castile, the mother of Catherine of Aragon. This particular monarch saw fit to gird her swelling loins with armour, rally her forces and ride into battle, lumpy but loyal, when she was a full eight months gone.

Doubtless Mr George Pinker, the present Queen's gynaecologist, had this lady in mind when he advised Princess Anne to give up riding for the last four months of her first pregnancy. Riding even the most docile of nags can unseat the mother – to say nothing of the babe within – likewise any form of movement that entails bumping and buffeting; royal mothers these days never fly when pregnant. Charles I's queen, Henrietta Maria's gaggle of female attendants, French like herself, swore that the causes of the queen's first miscarriage were the rickety royal carriages and the impossible English roads.

A sensible amount of exercise has always been advised. Apart from riding, the most common form of exercise indulged in by royal ladies was dancing. The therapeutic value of a gentle gavotte was not denied and George III's Queen, Charlotte, expecting her eighth child at any moment, danced indefatigably for most of the night with the French ambassador in the ballroom of St James's before being brought to bed in the early hours and safely delivered of a daughter. But Queen Charlotte, it must be remembered, produced babies as easily as shelling peas and almost as casually. Poor Mary of Modena, second wife of James II, was not so fortunate. By the time she reached the throne she had had eight pregnancies, all of them coming to nothing. She had lost one child, it is said, because of her enthusiastic efforts to master the latest dance craze, a style of gymnastic quadrille recently imported from France. She should have paid more heed to the lessons of history. A century and a half earlier Henry VIII had given Anne Boleyn special dispensation from taking part in the court revels on the death of his first wife, Catherine of Aragon, for Anne at the time was in an advanced state of pregnancy. As it turned out the dispensation did not avail Mistress Boleyn one whit. Two weeks after the celebrations the Queen swooned on hearing that Henry had been thrown from his horse in Windsor Great Park. Within forty-eight hours the Queen had lost her second child, and her fate was sealed.

Clothes worn during pregnancy in the past were not the loose, easy garments favoured by today's royal mothers. They differed little in style or size from ordinary female apparel because of the emphasis placed on severely restrictive undergarments. It was thought to be essential as late as the nineteenth century to bolster up a swelling stomach with stays and whalebone corsets, for if the womb was allowed to sag the child would be born hideously misshapen. It was this reasoning that also prompted the wearing of swaddling clothes for the newly born infant. Mary Queen of Scots, who adored being pregnant and skittishly ordered gold and silver buckets for her nursery and whole new wardrobes of velvet gowns for her midwife, had her own maternity dresses made with twenty-two inch waists and continued to wear them in her eighth month. Even allowing for the fact that the Scottish Queen normally had a sixteen-inch waist, the extra six inches cannot have left much slack. It is little wonder that James I was an odd-looking child.

Today's royal mothers are advised to lie low for the latter part of their pregnancies not, one suspects, entirely for reasons of health but because, no matter how skilful the design, a fully extended maternity dress is not a regal garment. Princess Michael of Kent, the most accessible and gregarious of the present Royal Family, is always reluctant to leave the limelight but admits that being six foot tall and heavily pregnant is not the easiest condition in which to plant a tree or launch a submarine.

The riveting question of the gender of the babe-to-be, with kingdoms and empires at stake, was an all-consuming subject for discussion. There were a hundred different 'foolproof' ways of determining which sex the child would be. The fifteenth-century *Babees Boke* states unequivocally that if a woman had a good colour, a bright eye and a constant body temperature, she was carrying a son. If her face was pale in colour and spotted with red, if she felt lumpen and sluggish, her eyes lacklustre, her disposition fretful and melancholic, her spirits low, she was not only an unattractive sight and a wretched companion, but worse, she could expect a daughter. As to diet, salt and salted foods were to be eschewed because these would clog the baby's vital passages. Delicate fare that would encourage a blooming complexion in the child was best. Peaches were Jane Seymour's craving, apples Queen Charlotte's. The homely pudding we know as apple charlotte is supposed to have been the Queen's recipe, invented when carrying her sixth child. It is a stodgy combination of apples, sugar, bread, and cinnamon but its salutary properties in the light of Queen Charlotte's large healthy family cannot be gainsaid.

By the beginning of the nineteenth century medicine, and especially obstetrics, had progressed so far that ante-natal advice, aside from drugs, was not much different from that offered in family clinics today. Richard Croft, the obstetrician who supervised Princess Charlotte's confinement, had some plain good sense to offer. For Charlotte he drew up a kind of list of school rules. She should eat only plainly cooked food that was easy to digest, no sauces or rich puddings or stodge like her grandmother's apple special. She should keep herself clean by sponging her limbs in tepid water every day and by taking a warm, shallow bath every second day. She should exercise regularly, a little walking or gentle riding if the weather permitted (inevitably, in the company of princesses, we are back to horses).

Another popular royal sport, particularly in Victorian days, was skating. It was skating that almost did for the Duke of Clarence, first-born of Edward Prince of Wales and his wife Alexandra. The Princess, seven months gone, had driven out to Windsor with her husband to join an afternoon skating party in the Great Park. Suddenly she felt dizzy, swooned, and had to be carried back to the castle where later than evening Prince Albert Victor, 'Eddy', was born. He weighed little more than three pounds. His mother thought the whole business a great joke. Because of the totally unexpected turn of events there were no preparations for the child's arrival. The baby was wrapped in a flannel petticoat instead of the dainty layette which was at home in London. The Princess laughed unconcernedly. Her mother-in-law was not amused.

Anthony van Dyck's portrait of Henrietta Maria, Charles II's Queen, showing the concessions that she made in her dress to cope with her pregnancy

The most common form of exercise adopted by modern princesses is doing up their houses. In some cases they literally do it themselves. Princess Michael, for one, is a professional interior decorator and was busy hanging large family portraits in her Kensington Palace home when six months pregnant with Lord Frederick. Climbing ladders is not an approved ante-natal activity but possibly Princess Michael, Austrian-born and built like Brunnhilde, did not need one. The Queen was in the process of modernizing Clarence House when she was expecting Princess Anne and threw herself into the business of choosing paint and papers with gusto. The nursery was not completed by the time Princess Anne was born, and for the first months of her life Anne slept in a crib in her father's dressing room.

Experts tell us now that there is often a flurry of activity from the expectant mother just before she gives birth. Whether this is some vestigial nest-building exercise or merely an attempt to do all those things that the new-born will inhibit is a matter for speculation, and irrelevant at that, beside the event of the birth itself.

II

Brought to Bed

'The Princess Anne Mrs Mark Phillips was safely delivered of a son at St Mary's Hospital Paddington at 10.46 today. Her Royal Highness and her son are both doing well.'

It all sounds so easy now – 'safely delivered', 'both doing well'. Not as romantic as the lying-in chamber at Hampton Court maybe, where Jane Seymour gave birth to the future Edward VI in her room of crimson silk hangings and finely worked tapestries. But a great deal safer. Before plunging pell mell into the Chamber of Horrors that passed for a delivery room in the not so very distant past, let us first don surgical masks and freshly laundered, sterilized gowns with St Mary's Hospital Paddington laundry marks, and see how our horsy heroine Mrs Mark Phillips made out five years ago on young Peter's birthday.

The Princess arrived by car, the gallant captain himself at the wheel, in Praed Street, an unprepossessing thoroughfare lined with sandwich bars, shops, and cheap hotels hard by Paddington Mainline Station, the previous evening. They came to the side entrance to the Lindo Wing, the private sector of the hospital, and were received by a small boarding party of nurses and junior doctors. The Princess, her hair casually knotted in a ponytail, was in high spirits. She cracked jokes about shedding her load at long last. The captain, with his usual embarrassed, ever-smiling diffidence, was shown to a waiting room where he thumbed through back numbers of *The Field* and *Country Life*. Meanwhile,

33

his wife, in much the same way as an airline pilot goes through his checklist before a long haul, embarked on the usual pre-birth check-ups. Temperature, blood pressure, enema, warm bath. Then finally into a plain, white nightgown fastened at the back with tapes before being helped into the high, iron hospital bed. The room is small with plain, white walls, blue curtains to match the bedspread, a colour television (where later she can watch *Blue Peter*, one of her favourite programmes), a couple of rather uncomfortable straight-backed chairs, and a washbasin in one corner.

'Gosh, I feel knackered already and it hasn't even started,' says our heroine, flopping back onto the pillows.

Enter Mr Pinker. George Douglas Pinker, the Queen's gynaecologist, is exactly the sort of doctor figure with which romantic novels about hospital courtships are peopled. Tall, handsome, greying at the temples, he would make a fortune giving lessons in The Bedside Manner. He is courteous without being deferential, friendly but never familiar. He is also amazingly thoughtful. Four years previously, before performing an emergency Caesarian section on the Duchess of Gloucester on the birth of her first child, he did not forget to telephone his wife, Dorothy, at their home in fashionable, tree-lined Kingston Hill to say he would be late for dinner.

'Well now Mrs Phillips, my dear. What is it going to be?' he says, pretending to consult the royal notes hanging from a clipboard at the bottom of the bed. 'Boy or girl?'

The Princess says she supposes that being the first grandchild and that, it would be nice to have a boy, but speaking personally she doesn't give a hoot so long as the baby has ten fingers and ten toes. The nurses smile indulgently as if this is the first time they have ever heard such a notion. Mr Pinker, who has four grown-up children of his own, pats her legs reassuringly and says that everything is just fine and he'll be back soon.

Now it is time to strap on all the hardware that goes with monitoring the progress of the unborn child from the first stages of labour to its final sortie through the birth canal. The monitor is a highly sophisticated and extremely expensive machine (at the time St Mary's only had four altogether) which resembles a television stuck on top of a portable barbecue.

'I hope my hands aren't too cold,' says Sister, hoisting up the

Princess Anne, expecting her second child, walking round the cross-country course at the Badminton Horse Trials in 1981

royal nightdress as discreetly as possible. Captain Phillips has been despatched to the reading room again for another dose of *Country Life*. 'We've just got to get these straps fitted round your tum.' It is not easy. Our heroine is a grand, healthy, large-boned lassie and even when not nine months gone, she would be tricky to budge. It takes two nurses a little while to manipulate and manoeuvre the vast pink belly that looks uncannily like a family-sized oven-ready turkey.

'I say, isn't it a bit tight?' she asks a trifle breathlessly.

'Honestly, three-day eventing at Burghley is a doddle compared to this.'

'It has to be fairly tight or we shan't pick up baby's heartbeat,' explains Sister soothingly. As a royal watcher for many years she knows that her patient can cut up rough. 'Now then, is that better?' She smooths down the sheet, adjusts the cover. 'I think we can ask Captain Phillips to come back in. I'm sure he'd like to see what baby's up to.'

Re-enter Mark carrying a copy of *Horse and Hound*.

'I say old thing,' he says looking nervously at his wife harnessed to the portable barbecue. 'Are you all right? You look miffed.'

And so for the next few hours, just like all those other expectant parents upstairs in the ordinary public maternity wards, where the nurses' hands are as cold and the rubber straps as irritating, the Princess and her husband chat and laugh and watch the extraordinary series of patterns on the television screen, signifying the foetal movements and listen to the strange underwater gurglings that represent the foetal heart and prove that junior is still fighting fit and ready to roll.

For a first baby it was a short labour, a mere seven hours, much of that anaesthetized by an epidural injection in the spine which numbs the lower part of the body. Captain Phillips stayed with his wife throughout. Mr Pinker tactfully positioned him at the top of the bed, away from the gory details, where he clutched his wife's hand and encouraged her to push at the appropriate time. As soon as the baby had been washed and dressed in its own hospital nightgown Princess Anne telephoned her mother at Buckingham Palace. The Queen was so absorbed in the child, the size, the shape, the weight and whom he took after, that she broke the tradition of royal protocol by arriving eight minutes late for a Palace investiture. The waiting audience clapped enthusiastically when they heard Granny's good news. Babies have the same effect as raspberries and sunshine. Princess Anne in the meantime settled back with her second post-natal cup of sweet, lukewarm, St Mary's special tea and gazed mistily at the bundle beside her. St Mary's cradles have convenient see-through sides and the same steering principle as supermarket trolleys.

The chances of Prince Charles attending the birth of his first child are high. Even before the Princess's pregnancy was officially announced, Charles was throwing out hints that, unlike his own

Opposite: *Buckingham Palace's announcement of the birth of Peter Phillips at St Mary's Paddington on 15 November 1977, signed by George Pinker, the Queen's gynaecologist*

BUCKINGHAM PALACE

Her Royal Highness The Princess Anne, Mrs Mark Phillips
was safely delivered of a son at St. Mary's Hospital,
Paddington at *10.46 AM* today.

Her Royal Highness and her son are both doing well.

Signed. *M.E.Bayliss.*

C. A. Chatte..

DR Harvey

George Pinker

15th November, 1977.

father, who was playing squash with his equerry when the Duchess of Edinburgh was giving birth to her eldest son, he wanted to be present for the great event. During the young newly-weds' strenuous whistle-stop tour of Wales, their first official tour as Prince and Princess of that country, they visited a hospital and spent some time chatting to a young mother who had just had her first child with her husband standing by. Prince Charles said he thought it was a jolly good idea for husbands to be around to give moral support to their wives. The Princess smiled her shy smile, but said nothing. The likelihood of the birth taking place at St Mary's Paddington is also high. George Pinker is a firm believer in the advisability of hospitals, not homes, for most deliveries, especially the first.

But neither Charles nor Diana was born in a hospital. Charles was born in Buckingham Palace in a bedroom converted temporarily into a labour ward. Diana was born at Park House, the sprawling ten-bedroomed Victorian pile adjoining the royal estate at Sandringham which had been lent to her father, then Viscount Althorp, and his first wife Frances, daughter of Lord Fermoy. It was, thankfully, an uncomplicated delivery. The previous year the Althorps' first son, John, named after his father, had died only ten hours after his birth and Viscountess Althorp had taken the baby's death very hard. Any small regret that she may have had on producing a third daughter was immediately dispelled at the sight of the new baby who weighed a healthy 7lb 12 oz and never stopped smiling, according to reports from the nursery staff at Park House. Baby Diana spent the first six months of her life in the Althorp family cradle which had been used for her two older sisters Sarah and Jane. It was a typical old-fashioned nursery-rhyme cradle with lace curtains fringed with *broderie anglaise* and a huge, white, satin ribbon hanging down from the centre of the headcover. It was prettily refurbished for the new arrival with new curtains and ribbon, the material sprigged with pale pink rosebuds and a quilt cover to match. Diana inherited most of the exquisitely embroidered babyclothes that her older sisters had worn. Her mother's favourite was a stiff white party dress festooned with lace ruffles and a welter of underskirts which the little girl wore for her first birthday party. All the sisters were exceptionally pretty babies with their curling, yellow hair and cornflower blue eyes, but of the three it was Diana who had the sort of looks that win baby competitions. A friend of her mother's once jokingly suggested that Frances should enter her third-born for the local baby beauty contest at the Sandringham summer fete. Lady Althorp shuddered at the thought and murmured 'over my dead body'.

Safe, clinical, private. Today's royal mothers can expect their confinements to be all of these. Set the clock back three hundred years and almost exactly the opposite conditions prevail. But what is so private, you ask, about fifty international pressmen and as many photographers laying siege to the entrance of the Lindo Wing back there in November 1977 for news of the Queen's first grandchild? For all it affected the Princess herself it could have been treble that number. St Mary's Paddington is used to handling the press. Three months earlier the pop singer Lulu had had a baby in the Lindo Wing and the baby-besotted press came in droves. In any case, Princess Anne thrived on visitors bearing flowers, fruit, and woolly bootees. There was only one gate-crasher. An intrepid girl reporter, despatched from a news-desk to get the obligatory royal-bundle-of-joy story, borrowed a Hermès scarf, knotted it at the tip of her chin in time-honoured point-to-point tradition, bought three dozen red roses, and slipped in unnoticed with a group of official visitors. She actually made it to the Princess's room before being discovered and booted out. But she was there long enough to reveal to a breathless waiting world her first-hand, exclusive, eye-witness report, namely that Mrs Phillips and baby, as far as she could see through the jungle of flowers, were both doing well.

Privacy as we have already seen was not something that royals in the past were either accustomed to or desired. It was not in their interests to be private. When producing an heir was tantamount to keeping your head on your shoulders it was in a family's interest to make sure that the birth was as well publicized as possible. Nowhere was this more evident than at the birth of James Francis Edward Stuart (later dubbed the Old Pretender) in June 1688. Thanks to the foresight of a bored bystander, who whiled away the waiting hours by taking a headcount, we know that there were sixty-seven people present in the royal bedchamber of St James's

Princess Anne and Captain Mark Phillips leaving the Lindo Wing of St Mary's Paddington with their first baby, Peter

Palace when the Queen, Mary Beatrice of Modena, James II's second wife, was brought to bed. Admittedly, this was a special-category birth. Not only the dynasty but the Catholic supremacy depended on the outcome of her lying-in. Her merry brother-in-law, Charles, had had a score of bastard children wailing in the royal nursery, but no legitimate successor.

Stuart Queens, as we have seen, had a singularly depressing success rate as far as babies were concerned. Mary Beatrice should have been an odds-on favourite, for when she married James she was only seventeen with at least twenty good child-bearing years before her. But alas, it did not work out as easily as James had hoped. His seventeen-year-old convent girl, despite her buxom figure, her wide hips, and long, strong legs, miscarried well before her time or else produced such puny offspring that they all died of smallpox or measles or convulsions before they had left the cradle. James grew morose, sent his wife off to Bath and called in a gaggle of doctors with strange remedies to tackle the delicate and by now pressing problem. When at last Mary became pregnant for the ninth time he declared the day a public holiday and the priests said special prayers for the safety of the Queen and her child in churches throughout the realm.

When her labour started the Queen immediately sent a message to the King, who had been playing cards until the small hours, that he must quickly call for witnesses. As if by some secret prearranged signal, like the beating of a dinner gong, all sorts of officials, attendants, ladies-in-waiting, heralds, and hangers-on raced towards the lying-in chamber. Fortunately it was a large room. It was also a long labour so that the sixty-seven witnesses, jostling for prime viewing space at the foot of the great four-poster to make sure no mischief was done, had time to eat and drink and gossip and even play cards while they waited. In France, incidentally, the publicity surrounding royal births was even worse. The lying-in chamber used by Marie Antoinette was more like a public square with a motorway at one end, along which an endless stream of curious people passed. Pregnant purists who complain that having a baby in hospital these days with medical students peering and student nurses pummelling is a degrading ordeal should spare a thought for the royal mothers of the past.

But we were waiting in St James's Palace for Mary to come good. The contractions grew stronger and more frequent. The moans became screams, the screams turned to shrieks. The watchful sixty-seven closed ranks for the final act when, much to everyone's fury and frustration, Mrs Judith Wilkes the midwife drew the curtain at the foot of the bed and blocked out the view. It was now that the first whispers of sleight of hand were nurtured with dark hints that a substitute child had been smuggled into the room to replace a stillborn child. The story went that the intruder had been introduced into the royal bed in a warming pan. There was certainly a warming pan in the royal bed before the Queen started labour (heaven knows why, because this was June). It sounds improbable, but not impossible, for seventeenth-century warming pans were not the flat, stream-lined brass affairs so popular as tea-room furnishing today. They were deep, round and capacious with lids that could be left slightly ajar. A neatly parcelled child, tightly swaddled and of average birth size, say six pounds, could easily have been secreted inside one of these with the lid open to allow it to breathe.

A Dutch satirical cartoon concerning the birth of James Francis Stuart, the Old Pretender, in June 1688. The nurse is shown carrying a moneybag, implying bribery, while the baby is holding a windmill because his father was reputed to be a miller. James II is peeping through the curtain's behind the Queen's head, while she is surrounded by papal agents

Mrs Wilkes could not completely curtain off her mistress for the accoucheuse needed a certain amount of room to move in. Grudgingly, she left a chink in the hangings at the side of the bed. Because of the crucial importance of this particular infant, James had devised an elaborate plan whereby he would know at once what sex the child was. It would not, he felt, have been seemly for him to cry out 'What is it, tell me quick? Boy or girl?' The King, unlike Captain Phillips, was not clutching his wife's hand at the top of the bed in her hour of need, but standing some distance away on the far side of the room chatting to the Lord Chancellor.

They were probably discussing affairs of state since the Lord Chamberlain, the Privy Seal, and the entire Privy Council were also present. The Dowager Queen Catherine was one of the last to arrive and was standing beside the clock. The plan was this. If the baby was a boy Mrs Wilkes, from her prime position next to the stage, was to pull at the hem of her dress twice. This innocent gesture would be picked up by Lady Sunderland, a faithful retainer, also a Catholic, in the second row of the stalls and she would then pat the side of her head, thus alerting the Monarch at the back of the dress circle that a male heir had arrived. At just after ten in the morning the Queen shrieked 'Oh you kill me, you kill me,' gave three mighty shoves, and the baby emerged. James was so beside himself with excitement that he completely forgot the prearranged signal and called out over the heads of the assembly.

'What is it?'.

'What your Majesty desires,' came the reply from a Lady of the Bedchamber who could see more of the action, whereupon a passing earl stole the show by clearing a path through the mêlée and crying 'Make way for the Prince!'

The chances of there being a switch are pretty remote. Many of the attendant women, Mrs Dawson for one, were Protestants with vested interests who were watching the proceedings like hawks to make sure there was no monkey business. It was a Sunday morning and a lot of the witnesses had had to be fetched from their devotions. One notable absentee in this bizarre event was the official royal accoucheur Hugh Chamberlen, one of the famous forceps Chamberlens of whom we shall hear more anon. He had been called away urgently to a case in Chatham and unfortunately missed out on all the prizes the delighted monarch dished out straight after James Francis Edward's arrival. Dr Waldegrave, the royal physician, received a knighthood and the pious Mrs Wilkes was given five hundred guineas with which, said the King, she could buy herself some breakfast.

It would all have been very different if the child had been a girl. Princes have always been preferred to princesses. When Queen Victoria's obstetrician, Dr Locock, announced with understandable apprehension after the birth of the sovereign's first child, 'Oh Madam, it is a princess,' the witness in the chamber heard the Queen reply drily, 'Never mind. Next time it will be a prince.' When the present Queen, then the young Duchess of Edinburgh, was carrying her first-born she made no secret of the fact that she wanted a boy. And when Charles duly arrived the fountains in Trafalgar Square ran blue for three days and twelve extra secretaries were taken onto the Buckingham Palace payroll to cope with the flood of telegrams, letters, an gifts that followed his birth. In medieval Italy black flags were hung out in the streets and squares when a royal princess was born to signify the public disappointment. George II, impatient to be off and have a jolly time on the battlefield instead of hanging about at court learning to dance, was coldly informed by his father that he must first sire a son. No male child, no battles. So convinced was Henry VIII that Anne Boleyn would provide him with a son that the official notices announcing the birth of a new prince were written out in advance. When instead the baby Elizabeth was born the notices had to be hastily amended and a final 's' added to the word 'Prince'. Some of the notices had already been despatched so the 's' was never added. When the midwife told Henry the news, he flushed with anger and chewed on his lip and had to be persuaded to carry the baby to the window to show to the crowds waiting outside the Palace at Greenwich. He refused to attend Elizabeth's christening and shamelessly delegated all responsibility for her as a child.

Boy babies were lavished with presents. Elizabeth, apparently understanding her own father's discrimination against her, was wildly generous to her male godchildren. One of her favourite godsons was Henry, elder son of James VI of Scotland and his wife Anne of Denmark. His christening gifts from the English monarch included a cupboard full of plate and a stack of gold goblets which were so heavy that it took two men to carry them into the christening chamber.

In war-torn medieval France the birth of a boy was proclaimed by the town crier as another small defender of *la patrie*. Women's liberationists will be delighted to hear that our new Princess of Wales is as dotty about little girls as little boys and has said that she honestly doesn't mind which she has first. If anything, said a former colleague, a nursery-school teacher who worked alongside Lady Diana, she prefers girls. She used to say she couldn't wait for a row of small girls in identical Laura Ashley dresses, so much more fun to play with than grubby little boys in sneakers.

One place where males were definitely *not* preferred was the delivery room. Indeed, obstetrics as a science lagged far behind the other branches of medicine for the very reason that until the end of the sixteenth century men were not allowed to attend confinements. The wretched doctors were not even allowed to witness their own wives' deliveries. One desperate medic in the fourteenth century is recorded as having crawled into his bedroom on hands and knees in order to get a sneaking idea of the miracle of birth and, having seen it, crawled out again. There were exceptions to this. If for instance the baby was considered to be important enough to have its horoscope cast, an astrologer would be allowed in, but stationed at a discreet distance. Similarly, if the mother raved and shrieked more than was thought normal during her labour a priest might be summoned to perform an exorcism, for the woman must surely have been possessed of devils. It was not only in England that men were banned from births. In Germany in 1552 a certain Dr Wertt of Hamburg became so frustrated at having to depend for all his medical information in the field of obstetrics on some dotty old midwife that he resolved to see things for himself. He dressed himself in a gown and midwife's apron, tied a scarf over his head, and presented himself at the next lying-in. Unfortunately, his disguise failed. The hapless transvestite was dragged from the room and publicly burned.

As for those ancient midwives, they had a perfectly ghastly collection of obstetric tools more suited to a torture chamber than a delivery room. There was a whole collection of bone and metal instruments which were used for prising a tardy child out of its mother's womb. One of these was the *vectis*, an instrument with a curving blade which was lodged as gently as possible on one side of the emerging infant's head and used as a sort of lever to prise it out. The whole exercise was a bit like retrieving something lost down a drain. There were all sorts of tools which could, with difficulty and terrible agony to the mother, be attached round some part of the child, leg, ear, chin, to assist the birth. Less gruesome was the fillet, a length of silk or leather or woollen material which the midwife attempted to wrap round the recalcitrant infant's head or nose or any protruding part. It was a pretty difficult manoeuvre and midwives with small hands were obviously better at this. Fillets were handiest for breach births since it was easier to hook the material round the child's ankle, but the pain for the mother must have been unspeakable.

45

Crowds outside Buckingham Palace, celebrating the news of the birth of Prince Charles on 14 November 1948

Anaesthetics were not in use until the mid-nineteenth century. Queen Victoria allowed small quantities of chloroform to be dropped onto a handkerchief to relieve her when she was having Prince Leopold. But before that the only painkillers were herbs such as mandragora, crushed and made into a tea, or alcohol. Many a baby was born to a tipsy mother, too drunk to enquire much after the baby's sex or condition.

Should all the digging and prodding and poking and filleting fail to produce the goods, more drastic measures were taken. It was not unusual for a woman experiencing a prolonged labour to be laid on a blanket and tossed in the air or even dunked into a cold bath to shock her into expelling the child. Shock was a favourite tactic. Give a woman in labour a few sharp slaps or a couple of hard pokes in the ribs and she might recognize that speed was of the essence. In some cases flogging was recommended and executed. Since it was not appropriate to flog ladies of gentle birth and high rank, a curious variation on the flogging theme was occasionally practised. There is a story of a German Empress in the fifteenth century who spent some thirty-six hours of useless pushing. To shock her into her senses twenty-four wretched men were brought into the chamber and flogged in front of her. Two of the poor fellows were actually flogged to death before the Empress eventually produced the baby. Whether it was the fatal flogging or the sight of men in her chamber that produced the baby is not clear. And then came the Great Breakthrough. Into the bedlam of blanket tossing and flogging rode the cavalry in the shape of the Chamberlens.

The Chamberlens were a refugee Huguenot family who had fled from the persecutions in France to England at the end of the sixteenth century, bringing with them their amazing New Technology, the obstretic forceps. There is mention of instruments similar to forceps in Arab medicine as early as 1000 A.D., but the Chamberlens claimed to own the patent. Their forceps were a heavier and cruder version of today's instruments, built on the sugar-tong principle with large, circular handles and long, curving blades. The Chamberlens soon became a by-word for easy labour in fashionable circles and their services were called for by all the grand families including, of course, the royals. Peter Chamberlen supervised the lying-in of Charles I's consort, Queen Henrietta Maria. His son Hugh was the absentee accoucheur who should have attended the birth of the Old Pretender. He also supervised the unsuccessful deliveries of the progeny of the last two Stuart Queens, Mary and Anne.

To protect their invention the Chamberlens adopted the most extraordinary cloak-and-dagger tactics. If it was decided that forceps were necessary to assist a particular delivery, a message went out and the burlesque began. Two large mysterious men would enter the room carrying between them one large mysterious chest, about the size and shape of a cabin trunk with the lid firmly battened down. This would be placed with great care beside the bed as if it contained a cargo of Meissen or Ming. Everyone but the accoucheur would then be sent packing and the patient herself would have her eyes blindfolded. Heaven only knows what she imagined the box to contain. But though the use of forceps undoubtedly made the majority of births simpler and less agonizing for the mother, there were still many cases where they were useless. This was an age when rickets was still a common condition, often resulting in hideous curvatures of the spine and the pelvis which made childbearing a risky and, more often than not, fatal undertaking. In 1670 Hugh Chamberlen took his magic box to France in the hope of selling the copyright for vast sums of money to the famous French obstetrician Mauriceau. 'Sure, I'll have a look at them', says the wily Frenchman, but first would the good Dr Chamberlen see what he and his magic tongs could make of one of Mauriceau's more complicated patients, a dwarf mother horribly misshapen by rickets. Smelling a sale, Dr Chamberlen declared recklessly that all he needed was fifteen minutes in the little lady's chamber and the child would be born. In fact, he spent three hours desperately poking and pulling to no avail. In the end they had to give her a Caesarian operation and both mother and child died.

But even forceps fell victim to changing fashion and, just as rockers on babies' cradles in the nineteenth century were considered to be extremely damaging to small infant limbs and brains, so forceps at around the same time were virtually written off as a dangerous old-fashioned practice. Probably the biggest victim of this advanced way of thinking was Princess Charlotte, only daughter of George IV, upon whom the Hanoverians were pinning all their hopes for an heir.

The circumstances surrounding the tragic death of Princess

Charlotte have been meticulously chronicled and every sad detail passed down to us as a grim reminder of what can happen even when the best advice is available. When the Princess became pregnant, her husband Prince Leopold of Saxe-Coburg requested a German doctor to attend his wife. He obviously didn't have much faith in the natives. He really wanted Stockmar, his personal adviser and physician, to attend her. But Stockmar, whose only medical experience had been acquired during his time in the army, had wisely declined to attend the Princess during her pregnancy. He may have had a premonition of disaster and thought that, being a foreigner, he would have been the first to carry the can. Leopold was, as usual, shouted down by his headstrong wife who instead engaged a Dr Baillie to attend to her ante-natal arrangements, assisted by a local woman from the village called Mrs Griffiths who had a string of successful deliveries under her apron. To reassure her husband that she was perfectly content and all was going smoothly, Charlotte re-engaged her favourite old nannie, Nottie, who came to live with them in Claremont Park near Woking in Surrey for the last few weeks of her pregnancy. Dr Baillie's methods, quite normal practice at the time, included frequent bleeding of his patient, an exercise which was thought to make the baby smaller and therefore easier to bear. Towards the end of her time, another doctor, the fashionable Sir Richard Croft, was appointed to attend her. Sir Richard was a society obstetrician used by all the ruling families and very highly regarded.

The Princess's labour began at seven in the evening on Monday, 3 November 1817 and was to last for more than fifty hours. The first stage took twenty-six hours to complete, which seems like a life-time in these days of labour-inducing drugs, but was not a rare occurrence at the time. The mystery is why Sir Richard did not see fit to use forceps to speed up the second stage. He dithered and delayed and, in the end, advised the increasingly anxious Leopold that in the circumstances word should be sent to the Prince Regent to come at once to his daughter's bedside. There then began a series of dreadful nightmare events which culminated in the failure of the Regent to reach Claremont in time to see his precious little girl before she died. For a start, he wasn't in London when the messengers arrived hotfoot from Surrey. He was visiting his mistress, Lady Hertford, and took the dickens of a long time to detach himself from her and return to Whitehall. He at once set out for Claremont, but was further delayed by the coach losing a wheel just beyond Richmond and by the dense fog

Cartoon showing the Prince Regent in bed with his mistress, Lady Hertford, when news reached him of the fear that his only daughter, Princess Charlotte, might well die in childbirth

which made speed impossible. Meanwhile, Charlotte had produced a huge stillborn son which no amount of artificial respiration, massaging of small, stiff limbs, hot baths, or spoonfuls of brandy poured into its mouth, would resuscitate. And now it seemed that worse was to follow, for the mother herself was in mortal danger. The placenta was removed with difficulty by hand and then the Princess fell into a sort of listlessness, showing no

51

desire to fight for her life. To ease her pain they plied her with glasses of hot wine which resulted in her getting drowsily delirious. She asked for kind Stockmar to come. When he arrived at her bedside she seized his hand and cried out piteously, 'Stocky, they have made me tipsy.' A little later, cradled in her husband's arms, she died.

Charlotte's prolonged and grisly demise is probably the *Titanic* in the ocean of royal obstetric history. In sharp contrast was the birth of the future Henry VIII in the royal Palace of Greenwich in 1491. He was the third child of Elizabeth of York, who had no trouble producing fine healthy children. At birth he was pronounced 'lusty and likely' by the midwife, the highest possible praise. 'Lusty' meant he was a big, bonny child, and 'likely' that he was likely to survive. So ecstatic were his parents at the birth of a second son that showers of gold coins were thrown out of the palace windows onto the heads of the crowds gathered below.

Henry went even further when his own first-born arrived. Catherine of Aragon gave birth to a son, Henry, in February 1511. The King held a huge, extravagant tournament at the Palace of Westminster to celebrate his son's birth, in which he personally took part as Noble Coeur Loyal. After the jousting came the feasting. Fifty whole oxen were roasted on spits, and special tapestries commissioned for the occasion were hung on the walls. The high point of the evening came when six young men and six young women, gorgeously attired in bejewelled fancy dress to look like Eastern potentates, were wheeled into the hall in a flower-decked float. An arbour had been placed on top of it from which they sprang and performed some exotic routines. The King was immensely pleased with the show; he was always fond of dressing up and used to torment his wife, Catherine of Aragon, and her pious Spanish ladies-in-waiting by bursting into her quarters with a gang of his friends dressed up as Robin Hood and his Merrie Men, forcing the wretched Queen and her women who were still abed and therefore naked, as was the custom, to dance with them, tickling them with their arrows and pinching their cold bottoms. At the young Henry's birthday tournament the King, overcome with the revels and very drunk, announced that all the precious jewels in the dancers' costumes should be shared out among the guests. He probably expected a polite round of applause at this unexpected largesse, but instead the assembled guests went mad

Verses on the much lamented Death of the Princess Charlotte of Wales,

who died the 6th of Novr 1817. In the 22nd Year of her Age.

Our much beloved Charlotte's no more,
Cut off is her flower and bloom,
And she who possessed our hearts
Now tenants the sacred tomb.

She is dead! whose name was so dear,
And left us a sorrowful band,
For the spot where we'd anchor'd our hopes
Is become as a desolate land.

Lament then Oh Britons lament,
And pray that our loss be her gain,
The gain of our favorite Princess
Who with Angels in Heaven may reign.

Such a thought even gladdens our hearts,
Religion superlative theme,
Oh, where shall our sorrowing cease,
If not in thy pure flowing stream.

But the prince and the peasant must die,
And render to God one and all,
An account of their deeds upon Earth,
From the palace een' down to the stall.

Let us hope then her Saviour through faith,
Will receive her sweet spirit above,
For surely such Graces as her's
Cannot fail, to be pleasing to God.

Cease to mourn then your favorite Princess,
Whose soul is ascended on high,
To receive the reward that awaits her
And all that so piously die.

Verses written to commemorate the death of Princess Charlotte in November 1817

The family of Henry VII and Elizabeth of York, painted after the Queen's death in childbirth. Behind the King kneel their sons, Arthur, Prince of Wales, Henry, Duke of York who ascended the throne as Henry VIII, and Edmund. Behind the Queen kneel their daughters, Margaret, who married James IV of Scotland, Elizabeth, Mary, who married Louis XII of France, and Catherine. Edmund and Elizabeth died as children while Catherine lived only a few hours

Henry VIII as Noble Coeur Loyal, *taking part in the Great Westminster Tournament to celebrate the birth of his son Henry in February 1511*

and ran amok, pulling the robes from the terrified Terpsichores and leaving the Great Hall in rather the same way as football supporters might leave a stadium when the home team has been trounced. Sadly the longed-for baby prince died nine days later; Catherine was never to present the King with another son.

There is no shortage of information about royal confinements. From the earliest times the chroniclers have noted down all the details. William the Conqueror's mother, Herleve, the sixteen-year-old tanner's daughter from Falaise in Normandy, told her midwife, as she laboured to produce our first Norman king, that the previous night she had dreamed that a huge oaktree was growing out of her belly whose branches spread out over France and across the channel to England. You wouldn't need to be a mystic to understand the significance of that particular portent. More signs and wonders were to follow. Herleve had a difficult time producing William and, as the midwives worked to ease the pain of afterbirth, William was laid on one side in a straw-lined crib. Here, records another chronicler, the new-born babe was seen to grab armfuls of straw and press them to his breast, a pressage of his future lust for power and possessions.

Before leaving the superstition and sorcery of the dark ages of childbirth and stepping into the comparatively enlightened era of the eighteenth century when doctors were taking obstetrics more seriously, let us for a brief golden interlude forget the violent and tragic examples of royal confinements and follow the first stages of a baby born normally, easily and joyfully. Childbirth in olden days had its credit side too. Provided a child was not at the receiving end of one of those sharp delivery hooks or being dragged, half-throttled by an embroidered lasso from its mother's womb, there were some delightful aspects to old-fashioned childbirth. Before obstetrics took on a noticeably scientific look, with the introductions of drugs and clinical hygiene, the basic procedures from the Middle Ages through to the eighteenth century were pretty much the same. Of course, it became more comfortable, less primitive, and the dresses of the midwives reflected the current fashion, but broadly speaking the immediate post-natal procedure followed similar lines.

Let us imagine we are unobserved observers at the birth of Edward II in 1284 at Caernarvon Castle in North Wales. The birth takes place in a beautiful oak-beamed bedroom whose doors open out onto a central courtyard with a fountain. It is, by medieval standards, a cosy room with a stone chimney set diagonally in one corner and woven hangings covering the timbered walls to produce further insulation. The floor is strewn with rushes and onto these crushed herbs have been scattered to sweeten the air. (The two strongest impressions that we, and our hypersensitive noses, would have had of medieval castle life would certainly have been the smell and the cold.) The herbs mask the pungent odours that inevitably accompany childbearing, and there are also bowls containing crushed jasmine, lavender, and pansies, and small brass pots with burning aromatic candles. A contemporary picture of a noble birth in the thirteenth century shows the midwives wearing high, horned headdresses, reminiscent of those ostentatious sporting trophies with which hunters later decorated their library walls.

As soon as the infant Edward has had his umbilical cord cut and knotted, the midwife rises from the low three-legged stool on which she has been sitting at the foot of the bed throughout the delivery, and wraps him in a receiving cloth. Ordinarily, this was just a strip of soft, white flannel, but in this case it is made of smooth linen embroidered with gold thread and bearing in one corner his father Longshanks' coat of arms three gold lions on a plain red background. The midwife relinquishes her responsibility over the child and returns to her supervision of Queen Eleanor, weary but well-pleased that she has done her royal duty and provided her husband with an heir. (Mercifully, she doesn't yet know what a useless heir he will prove to be.) Baby Edward is now the responsibility of his nurse who carries him over to the fire for the long and thorough cleaning-up process.

She settles herself down on the specially designed nursing chair, with its low wide seat and straight back to give support to the wet nurse, as she holds the child to her waist. The elaborate grooming is ready to begin. First she unblocks the child's nose, mouth, and ears very gently with her thumb and forefinger and sprinkles a little salt on his tongue and behind his ears to ward off evil spirits and bring good luck.

Now comes the bath. The child is unwrapped and held briefly in a wooden tub which has been placed close to the fire to retain its heat. There is a fearful tale of a tub heated over the flames, tested with the tip of the elbow, as usual, and then offered to the nurse as being just right. But what the conscientious water-tester forgot to feel was the base of the bath which, being in this case metal, scalded the poor infant to death. (This was not to be Edward's fate, at birth at any rate, though he met his end gruesomely enough.)

It is now that the nurse can fully examine the child lying in her hands in the flower-scented water. She remarks on his puny physique and sickly complexion and sends out for a quart of ale to be warmed and added to the water to fortify and toughen him up. Had he been a Saxon child he could have expected more brutal treatment. Saxon babies were generally born within earshot of the battlefield so that from the first the frenzy of warfare would penetrate their minds. They were then dunked several times in icy water to prove their virility and if, as often happened, a few failed to survive the ordeal, they were written off as weaklings who wouldn't have made the grade anyway if they had lived. So Edward splashes about in his beery bath and is then lifted out, dried, and afterwards rubbed all over with flavoured oils – jasmine in this case which was thought to improve muscle development. Aromatherapy, which is currently taking our

*Charles I and Henrietta Maria, with their two eldest children, Charles who became
Charles II, and Mary, who married William II of Orange, and was the mother of
William III of England*

twentieth-century beauty salons by storm, was common knowledge in the Middle Ages.

Beside the nursing chair on a small table are set out all the contemporary post-natal paraphernalia, a honeycomb, a pot of salt, sweet-smelling oils, more herbs – a children's nurse could well have produced a pudding at the same time. And warming by the fire are the baby's swaddling clothes, long pieces of soft, white cloth which look ominously like miniature winding sheets. Into these the baby is rolled like a mail-order carpet, the final piece of cloth being folded neatly over his head and pinned into place. To secure the parcel even more carefully, coloured braids would be criss-crossed over the swaddling cloth so that the final product was a bit like the top of a latticed tart. Nappy changing was a skilled business. And finally the nurse dips her finger into the honeycomb and rubs it gently over the child's tongue and round his gums to encourage him to suck, whereupon the time has come at last to hand him over to the wet nurse for his first drop of sustenance.

The Tudors preferred Greenwich Palace to any of the other homes for having their confinements, but Stuart Queens favoured St James's. Charles I's Queen, Henrietta Maria, started the fashion. She had intended to have her first baby at Greenwich, but was put off when her first pregnancy ended in a miscarriage. She had gone down to Greenwich seven months pregnant to see to the final arrangements of her lying-in. As she left the Palace and was walking through the gardens with her ladies to her carriage an angry dog raced up and snapped at her dress. The poor little Queen was terrified and collapsed shrieking into the arms of her gentlewomen. Later that day she miscarried and thereafter refused to go to Greenwich. From that time on she chose St James's for her confinements. Her particular craving during pregnancy was shellfish, encouraging a barrage of cockle, winkle, and whelk stalls that lined the route from St James's to Whitehall, and the fashion for eating shellfish became naturally established.

Her daughter-in-law, Catherine, had a similarly sad experience, but at St James's. Charles II was unhygienically fond of animals: the breed of spaniels that he always had frisking at his heels owes its name to him. He had a special, dog-proof fence consisting of a sort of metal grid built round his four-poster bed to prevent the dogs jumping up and fouling the sheets, burying their bones under the pillows, or tearing down the velvet hangings. His wife, unfortunately, didn't have the same protection in her chamber. She was lying in bed, pregnant for the first time, when a fox raced into her room, chased by the King's pack of hounds, and leaped into her bed for refuge. Catherine, hardly surprisingly, lost the baby.

Meanwhile, a century earlier up in Scotland Mary Queen of Scots was characteristically treating her forthcoming confinement in the manner of a grand theatrical production. She redecorated her bedroom, ordered thirty bolts of royal blue damask from Brussels for new bed hangings and a set of gold and silver buckets for the nursery. The baby's crib was decked out as a mini-replica of the Queen's own bed. The midwife was provided with a new dress for the occasion, black velvet with a jewelled bodice and seductive *décolleté* which wasn't particularly suited either to her clinical duties or to the draughty state of Edinburgh Castle. Of course, there would have been blazing fires in all the rooms, but as someone complained at the time, the heat burned you at the front while the icy draught still whistled at your back. When her labour began Mary's pain was so acute – remember her insistence on whittling her waist down to twenty-two inches when halfway through her pregnancy – that the midwife, following a popular belief of the time, ordered one of the ladies-in-waiting to lie down beside the Queen and simulate labour pains, thereby transferring the Queen's discomfort to herself. Thus the two women lay groaning and screeching together like a couple of scalded cats – it doesn't seem to have had much effect on Mary who later described the whole business as surely a foretaste of hell and damnation.

Few royal mothers can have experienced so undignified a birth preamble as Princess Augusta, of Saxe-Gotha, the wife of Frederick Prince of Wales. Expecting her first child, she was thrust into a carriage at Hampton Court when her labour began and then raced at great speed, without a ha'p'orth of consideration for her obvious discomfort, the twelve bumpy miles to St James's Palace. Her dreary young husband was determined that the child should be born in London and not at Hampton Court, under the roof of his detested parents, George ii and Queen Caroline.

Augusta of Saxe-Gotha, wife of Frederick, Prince of Wales, with three of their children and members of her household in 1739. The Princess is holding her daughter Augusta – the baby born en route *from Hampton Court to St James's Palace – while Prince George, later George III, and Prince Edward are supported by Lady Archibald Hamilton. On the left, holding Prince George's hat, is Mrs Herbert, who was governess to Princess Augusta and had care of the royal children, and on the right is the Princess's vice-chamberlain with his key of office*

It was an extraordinary and humiliating prelude to any birth. The fact that it was the Princess of Wales's maiden delivery makes it the more bizarre. But then eccentric behaviour on the part of sons, particularly the eldest sons of Hanoverian monarchs, was about par for the course. Without alerting the King or Queen, who were playing cribbage and ombre respectively in other parts of the Palace, Fred, as soon as the message came from the Princess's chambers that the waters had broken, summoned a coach and horses to be sent secretly to a rear courtyard. Then, aided and abetted by a team of ladies-in-waiting, an equerry, and even a dancing master, Augusta was shoved wailing and protesting into the coach and propped up on pillows and cushions. The party whipped up the horses and galloped off to St James's at break-neck speed. It was a traumatic experience for the poor frightened girl. So distressed was she on arrival that Fred ordered all the lights outside St James's to be put out while his wife was half-hoisted, half-lifted out of the carriage so that no one should witness her unseemly and, by now, extremely damp and messy condition. By all accounts a great deal of mopping up had to be done on the way to the bedroom and it was whispered afterwards that her arrival took the staff so completely by surprise that no proper bed linen could be found and the royal bed was hastily made up with tablecloths. It was a tribute to Augusta's tough German ancestry and sturdy physique that both she and her infant, a daughter to be called Augusta after her mother, survived the ordeal. The Princess proved to be a prolific and uncomplicated procreator, and bore Fred nine children altogether.

Even more prolific than Augusta, and quite the jolliest royal mother in British history, was her daughter-in-law, Queen Charlotte. She stands out as some vast maternal mountain, constantly surrounded by children tugging at her skirts, sitting on her lap as she tried to get dressed in the mornings, playing football with her hats, and teetering around her bedroom in Buckingham House in her shoes. Queen Charlotte produced fifteen children in twenty-one years, of whom thirteen survived into adulthood. This remarkable record easily makes her Top Royal Rabbit, beating, by a distance, Edward III and Queen Philippa who produced seven sons and five daughters, of whom three died in infancy. Joint third are Victoria and Albert with nine, and the above-mentioned Fred and Augusta.

*Queen Charlotte, from a portrait painted by Benjamin West in 1779. Behind the
Queen are thirteen of her children on the terrace at Windsor Castle*

Benjamin West's painting showing the apotheosis of Prince Octavius being welcomed into heaven by his brother, Prince Alfred. Prince Alfred was the fourteenth child of Charlotte and George III and died in 1782 at the age of two. The following year their thirteenth child, Octavius, died at the age of four

According to the *Guinness Book of Feminine Achievements*, the all-time record for childbearing is held by a Russian lady, Madame Vassilet, of the nineteenth century who, in thirty confinements, produced the phenomenal sum of sixty-four children including eight sets of twins, seven sets of triplets, four sets of quads and the rest in single measures. No royal mother holds a candle to the creator of *that* crèche, though the Empress Maria Theresa had sixteen children and so did her son the Duke of Tuscany, while Cecily Neville, mother of Edward IV and Richard III, was the youngest of twenty-three children. Charlotte herself was the eighth of ten children and her great-grandfather had nineteen altogether, though admittedly by two wives.

The contemporary accounts of Charlotte's numerous births sound like the scenario for a musical comedy. She didn't seem to know the meaning of post-natal depression. Fortified by bracing prescriptions from Dr Hunter, the royal accoucheur, such as:

1 scruple of spirits of lemon
1½ scruples of compounded powder of contrayerva
1½ fluid ounces Alexiterial water
1½ fluid drams of nutmeg
½ a fluid dram of syrop of saffron

to be mixed and taken every six hours, she positively bounced with good health. Her favourite wet-nurse, Margaret Scott, would sit by the Queen's bedside with the latest royal addition on a velvet cushion on her lap and thus every afternoon the royal party would receive a troop of visitors. These were just curious and congratulatory members of the public who wanted to *see*, a little like those Leviathan queues that stretched along the Mall recently to view the Princess of Wales's wedding presents. They were admitted to the Queen's bedchamber at Buckingham House (only her first child was born at St James's) in groups of about forty at a time. They were offered seed cake and caudle, a frothy mixture not unlike flummery or zabaglione made from wine and eggs and sugar and said to work wonders for arthritis. The visits lasted for about two weeks and must have cost the Privy Purse a fortune since it was reckoned that five hundred pounds of cake were gobbled up every afternoon and eight gallons of caudle. Not since the lavish public hospitality of Charles I, who had eighty-six tables set up at Whitehall on special occasions and provided a running buffet of 7,000 roast sheep, 4,000 broiled chickens, and 1,500 spit-turned oxen, had the nation's stomach been so generously filled. William and Mary had been pretty fair trenchermen too with, it is said, a daily consumption at their private table of six bottles of claret, eight of champagne, three bottles of Spanish wine, and two bottles of Rhenish, but this was purely for their personal needs.

Queen Victoria, almost as prolific a breeder, was a far less enthusiastic one. She wrote in her diary that childbearing was the only thing she truly dreaded and was distinctly off-colour mentally as well as physically whenever she was approaching full term. While she was carrying her first child, an attempt was made to shoot her as she and Albert drove out one afternoon from Buckingham Palace along Constitution Hill. But, though the incident shocked her greatly, it had no dire effect on her pregnancy. It was Victoria who waived the tradition of having a scrum of witnesses in the delivery room. When Princess Vicky, the Princess Royal, was born the Queen limited the number of those actually present in the gold and white painted bedroom of the Palace to three: Dr Locock the accoucheur, Mrs Lilly the midwife, and dear Albert himself to hold her hand – 'a great comfort', she wrote later in her journal – during that first twelve-hour labour. In an adjoining room, with the door left discreetly ajar, waited the Queen's appointed witnesses – the Archbishop of Canterbury, the Bishop of London, the Prime Minister, the Foreign Secretary, the Home Secretary, and a few also-rans. Not even the Royal Physician himself, Sir James Clark, was required in the delivery room, but waited with a team of medical reserves in an antechamber in case of emergency.

And so we enter the twentieth century with its advanced obstetric methods, its sophisticated obstetric machinery, its clinical (some might say over-clinical) emphasis. We take it for granted that the present Queen was born by Caesarian section in 1926 (at the Duke and Duchess of York's private home at 11 Bruton Street), but a hundred years earlier the same operation would have had the almost inevitable result of failure, with the mother dying and probably the baby too. Until the end of the eighteenth century Caesarian operations were only carried out when the mother had died during labour and this was a last ditch and a desperate attempt to save the life of the child. The first

Princess Michael of Kent admiring her son, Lord Frederick Windsor, in a photograph taken by Lord Snowdon

successful Caesarian was performed in England by a doctor from Blackburn in 1793, but this seems to have been a fluke. In 1865 the Caesarian statistics were still appallingly grim: of the seventy-seven women on whom the operation had been performed, sixty-six of the mothers had died. Septicaemia was invariably the reason for death and it was not until the discovery of antibiotics well into this century that the operation became medically viable.

This stiffness, the formality, the ceremony has now totally vanished from royal confinements. When the Queen was closeted in the nursery of Buckingham Palace the Duke of Edinburgh was, as we have heard, playing squash with his equerry. Before the formal notice of the birth of an heir had been pinned to the railings of the Palace the word had already got out by a series of Chinese whispers via nurses, servants, and policemen to the waiting crowds. The birth of a prince or princess is now shared with the public as a domestic event rather than a constitutional achievement. Even royal mothers seem to have a healthy pragmatism about the whole business. When Prince Michael of Kent's son, Lord Frederick, was born, his mother exclaimed with delight, 'Look at his lovely big hands. He should make an excellent plumber.'

III

Received by the Church

The year was 1842. The principal godfather was Frederick William IV, the King of Prussia. The occasion was the christening of a prince in St George's Chapel, Windsor, which had been decorated with dozens of sprays of red and white and blue flowers threaded with silver ribbons. The procession which followed the baby into the church contained some two hundred dignitaries awash with ermine, and the baby's train was twenty feet long. This was, after all, the first male heir to be born to a British monarch for close to eighty years and Victoria and Albert, his delighted parents, were pushing the boat out. The baby was christened Albert Edward by the Archbishop of Canterbury – the titles of Prince of Wales, Duke of Cornwall, Duke of Rothesay, Earl of Carrick, Baron of Renfrew, Lord of the Isles, and Great Steward of Scotland were bestowed upon him. Afterwards a banquet was held for five hundred guests in Windsor Castle. Eight footmen carried in a vast silver punch-bowl designed by George IV, into which had been tipped 360 bottles of mulled wine with which the guests drank the baby's health. Afterwards a grand reception was held in the Waterloo Room, in the middle of which stood the christening cake, a colossal confection of sugar plums and silver bells, eight feet in diameter on the bottom tier and twelve feet high.

The lavish style and sense of occasion persisted for royal christenings up to and including that of the future Edward VIII in 1894. But this was probably the last of the Great British

The christening of Albert Edward, Prince of Wales, the eldest son of Victoria and Albert, which took place in St George's Chapel Windsor on 25 January 1842

Christenings. The Royal Family today prefer to keep their christenings small and private with only immediate relatives and the godparents attending. The last two generations of royal babies have been christened in the Music Room of Buckingham Palace, a much less spectacular setting than St James's Palace, Windsor Castle or Westminster Abbey, the traditional venues for royal baptism in the past. The most unpretentious and informal of the royals, the Gloucesters, delighted in having the simplest of services for their children. All three baby Gloucesters were christened in the local parish church at Barnwell near Peterborough in Northamptonshire, with the guests walking the short distance between the castle and the church.

For obvious reasons, christenings in olden days followed hard upon the birth of the child. With so many babies failing to survive the first few days, it was expedient to get them into the church as soon as possible. An unbaptized child would never get to heaven and in medieval times even midwives were allowed to baptize a child, if he or she looked too sickly to survive for more than a few hours. Edward VI, a pitifully weak specimen at birth, was christened at three days old, though in his case it was the mother, Jane Seymour, who died nine days later. It is usual these days to wait until the baby is about three months old before exposing it to the glare of publicity for the first time. Queen Victoria set the fashion for procrastination. She said flatly that before they were twelve weeks old all children – yes, even her own – looked like frogs. She was quite happy not to see them until they had improved and that wrinkled nut-like appearance had taken on a more human face. And with so many photographers in the Royal Family these days (even Captain Phillips is growing adept with his Kodak Instamatic and took some lovely snaps of his baby daughter's baptism) there is no denying that a smiling three-month-old makes a better subject than a squalling pickled nut.

By tradition, however, before the christening came the churching ceremony for the sanctification and purification of the mother who, it was thought, had been sullied not merely physically but also spiritually by the messy business of childbirth. Churching comes down to us from an ancient Hebrew custom and involved a good deal of splashing around in the waters of the Jordan in the original version. There were strict rules as to how the churching ceremony should be performed, from the robing of

72

*The Duke and Duchess of Gloucester with their elder son, the Earl of Ulster, at his
christening in the parish church at Barnwell in Northamptonshire*

the mother in her chamber to the blessing by the priest in the church. A schedule of events was prepared for the churching of Henry VII's Queen, Elizabeth of York, after her elder son Arthur was born, laying down a precise pecking order and timetable starting with her investiture in rich silks and laces by a duchess or a countess (whoever happened to be around at the time). She was then led ritualistically to the door of her chamber and ceremoniously passed on to a waiting duke and then on to the chapel.

Baptisms in the Middle Ages were comparatively simple, but reached two distinct peaks of magnificence and ostentation – including such props as regiments of heralds and gargantuan christening cakes – the first high point coming in the post-Renaissance period and the second in the pageant-loving late eighteenth and nineteenth centuries. The present fashion is for small intimate services followed by a sit-down lunch and a slice of fruit cake from Fortnum & Mason.

In the *dramatis personae* of medieval christenings a wardrobe mistress was an essential character, for the child would have to be painstakingly unswaddled before the dunking could be performed. For this purpose a small area was set aside near the font to be used as a changing room. It was comfortably equipped with carpet, cushions, and curtains, and here the chief lady-in-waiting would be handed the child to unwrap. It was not merely swaddling bands that had to come off, but also the odd assortment of strings, cords and stays that small babies were often tied into to keep their limbs straight. At last it was done and the naked and usually shrieking babe (medieval churches were not noted for their warmth) would be handed over to the priest. These were the times when superstitions were rife and salt would be rubbed into the child's ears and onto its tongue to represent the sacred gift bestowed upon it by the Holy Ghost. Oil would also be poured from a silver chalice onto the child's head. Now came the cold bath. Three times the unfortunate infant would be immersed up to its neck in the freezing water of the font. The water was, and by tradition still is, Holy Water from the Jordan. The font used by our present Royal Family is the gold, lily-shaped bath originally in St George's Chapel, Windsor, but now in Buckingham Palace. Scottish babies enjoyed a slight variation on this general theme and one which must have taken the chill off the occasion. A spoonful of whisky mixed with Scottish soil was placed on the child's tongue to remind him that he was descended from warrior stock and must grow up to be a worthy clansman. Prince Henry, the first-born son of James I and elder brother of Charles I, was christened in Holyrood Palace in a most solemn ceremony that was introduced by forty trumpeters and included a strange collection of Scottish chieftains carrying whisky, earth, jugs, basins, towels, and other washing tackle.

Now that the blue-blooded and by now goose-pimpled baby had been salted, oiled, soaked, and choked, all of which had miraculously made it into a proper little Christian, it was returned to the lady-in-waiting in the changing room who re-swaddled it and placed on its head, rather like a graduation mortar-board, a piece of white material the size of a table napkin. This was called a chrisom cloth and symbolized the child's new-found purity. All traces of original sin had been tipped out with the font water. The development from the plain square medieval chrisom cloth is another example of how much more elaborate christenings were to become. Tudor and Stuart chrisom cloths for noble and royal babies were richly embroidered and sewn with jewels: pearls were popular, as were rubies with a speck of coral for luck. Most babies object strongly to anything being put on their heads, least of all a prickly, heavy, jewel-encrusted headscarf. When Elizabeth Tudor was christened, her chrisom cloth, with its border of rubies and pearls, was carried by the Duchess of Norfolk; the Dowager Duchess carried the baby and the baby's magnificent purple velvet and ermine mantle was carried by three coroneted earls. For obscure, doubtless Freudian reasons, Scottish baby boys were dressed for the occasion in female clothes and vice-versa.

To make matters even more complicated, a lighted candle was placed either in the child's hand or in its godmother's hand and, at the same time, hundreds of torches would be lit along the walls of the church or chapel in public recognition of the child's new Christian status. And, by way of icing, a canopy was somehow hoisted over the baby, the candle, the godmother, the train, and the chrisom cloth. This was held at each corner by a nobleman and thus, ponderous as an elephant topped by a howdah, the procession would move slowly down the nave and into the blessed air.

At Charles II's christening in St James's Chapel the congregation looked like something out of a Busby Berkeley musical, since everyone had been asked to dress in crimson and white. The ladies wore white dresses, with crimson sashes, the men white cloaks and crimson stockings.

Comparable with the splendour of Edward vii's baptism was that of his namesake, Edward vi. For here at last was the Prince that Henry viii had moved heaven, earth, the Catholic Church, and the executioner's axe to obtain. W.K. Jordan, biographer of the boy King, describes the almost pagan pageantry of the over-blown occasion, with the King himself cast in the role of Arch Druid.

> The news of the birth of a prince was received with great rejoicing and festivities throughout the realm, but particularly in London where the bells were rung, 2,000 salvos were fired from the Tower, and a High Mass was sung at St Paul's, while ale and wine flowed in the streets for all to take. Plans were at once drawn, in which the King played an active role, for the christening of the infant on the third day after birth, a proclamation being issued dated October 12 which sternly forbade access to the court on the baptismal date because of the plague still epidemic in London . . . The protocols established by Margaret Beaufort for such functions were followed, requiring the Queen to receive perhaps as many as 400 guests while she was seated with the King on a state pallet, and then to observe the procession of the great clergy, the Council and the nobles, in that order, as the company moved into the Chapel where Cranmer performed the baptism. Edward was carried by the Marchioness of Exeter and the train of his robe by the Earl of Arundel, while Cranmer and Norfolk were godfathers at the font and Suffolk at the confirmation. Queen Jane throughout this long ordeal appeared reasonably well.

Appearances were deceptive. Queen Jane died from septicaemia twelve days after Edward was born.

Choosing godparents was a delicate and often dangerous business, for godparents were often picked more for political than for spiritual purposes. It was clearly expedient for James vi of Scotland to invite Elizabeth Tudor in the kingdom over the road to be godmother to his daughter Elizabeth, later the Winter

Queen. The baby was probably named after the English Queen to ingratiate the Stuarts even further with the Tudors, bearing in mind Elizabeth's childless condition and the likelihood of another throne to be inherited upon her death.

There were a number of superstitions regarding the selection of godparents. If a godmother was pregnant at the time of the baptism, either her godchild or her own child could expect to meet a violent and premature death. The luckiest godparent a child could have was the first poor person that the christening party ran into on the way to the church, for, according to the old maxim, a child with a poor stranger as his spiritual patron would live to a ripe old age and prosper during his life.

Political marriages between royals are no longer important and godparents also need not be chosen for reasons of diplomacy. Princess Anne chose racing-driver Jackie Stewart's wife, Helen, to

'The First of May', Winterhalter's painting of Prince Arthur with Queen Victoria in 1851. To celebrate the Prince's first birthday, his godfather, the Duke of Wellington, presents him with a casket

be her daughter's godmother simply because she is a close friend. The Stewarts have long been on close personal terms with Anne and Mark and often stay with them at Gatcombe, reciprocating this royal hospitality with invitations to visit their own home on the shores of Lake Geneva. And it was touching and also typical of the diffident, unassuming Prince Richard, Duke of Gloucester, to include among the plethora of distinguished godparents to his eldest son Alexander, Earl of Ulster, one of the partners in his architectural practice. The little Earl's other godparents include Princess Alexandra and Prince Charles and sundry other title-holders.

Godparents bring presents. Leading the field comfortably in sheer quantity were the coachloads of presents heaped on the infant Charles II. His mother Queen Henrietta Maria was still opening them a year after his birth. His most generous benefactor was one of the royal spinsters at his christening, the elderly and staggeringly wealthy Duchess of Richmond who gave the merry infant monarch £200 in coins and a jewel worth £7,000. Still not content that she had really done him proud, when Queen Henrietta Maria sent her own state coach with its retinue of coachmen, footmen, knights, and plumed horses to the Duchess's house in the Strand to carry her the short distance to St James's for the service, the obsequious old lady, by way of a gratuity, tipped each of the knights £50, the coachmen £20, and the running footmen £10 which must make it the most expensive taxi ride in history.

Prince Henry, Charles I's elder brother who died when he was eighteen, was given as a christening gift a parchment scroll from the Ambassador of Holland to the Scottish court, stating that a payment of five thousand florins was in the post for him. Less, one imagines, a token of Dutch natural affection for children than a diplomatic pay-off.

Nearly eighty years earlier Mary Tudor was given a tiny coral branch to be worn about her neck as a good luck charm, a present from her Spanish grandmother, Isabella of Castille, on her christening day. Baby rattles were often made of coral for the same superstitious reason. Other childish talismans to protect babies from witchcraft and sorcery were necklaces hung with dogs' teeth, preferably a bitch's who had just produced a litter. A hare's tooth was also deemed lucky and, if you could lay your hands on one, the ear of a vole would see you right. Donkeys were universally reckoned to be beasts of good fortune (remember the ass's milk) and a piece of donkey skin sewn into a sachet and tied about the child's person could only bring joy.

Numbers played an important part in these old superstitions. A child born at the eleventh hour should be baptized on the eleventh day of its life – you can almost see the midwife wagging her finger as she says it. The seventh-son-of-a-seventh-son legend and the mystical powers that such a child possesses are well-known and, with the ubiquitous tendency to large families in the un-pilled past, seventh sons were not uncommon. Kings and queens were more riddled with superstition than most, presumably because they had more at stake. Certain numbers had a significance for certain monarchs. James I was convinced that nineteen was a lucky number for his family and required that all his children be christened on that day of the month. When his second son Charles was born on 19 November 1600, he was so delighted and tickled by the coincidence that he waxed eloquent on the numbers game declaring,

> I first saw my wife on the 19th November on the coast of Norway, she bore my son Henry on the 19th February, my daughter Elizabeth on the 19th August and now she has given birth at Dunfermline to my second son on the anniversary of the day on which we first saw each other the 19th November, I being myself born on the 19th June.

This little homily passed over his wife's head for it was round about this time that Queen Anne started to drink heavily due to depression. She disapproved of the Scottish and English tradition of sending small children away from home to be looked after by wet-nurses and nannies. She wanted, but was not allowed, to look after them herself. She died in the not-so-lucky year 1619.

The children of today's royal parents are lavished with the usual collection of silver spoons, monogrammed christening mugs, and egg cups. Lord Frederick Windsor, Princess Michael's eldest, received from the Begum Aga Khan a beautiful Christian Dior romper suit of exquisite white lawn with feathery blue hand-embroidery, and a carved wooden rosary from his spiritual father, the Pope. The Princess is a Catholic and hung the gift on her son's

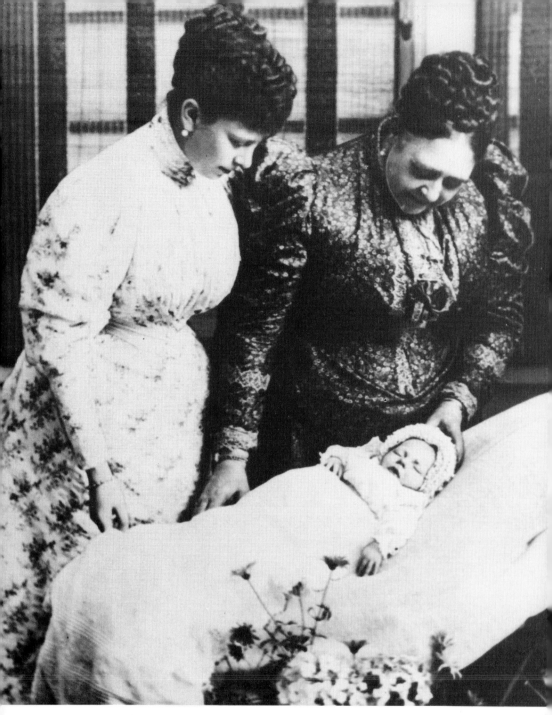

The infant Edward Albert Christian George Andrew Patrick David, being admired after his christening by his mother, Princess May, and his grandmother, the Duchess of Teck. Despite Queen Victoria's demand that he should be called Albert, the Prince was always known in the family as David

cradle. More of a family heirloom than a proper christening gift was the one-eared teddy bear handed down from Prince Richard of Gloucester to his son Alexander.

Naming their new babies is a subject on which royal parents have always had strong views. But for the stern disapproval of her paternal grandparents, King George v and Queen Mary, Princess Margaret would have been Princess Anne. When the Duchess of York suggested the name Anne as being rather pretty, back came the reply that Anne was not at all suitable and it was left over for the next generation. Names, like godparents, were chosen for reasons of diplomacy. By sticking in a fourth Christian name which happened to be that of your arch-rival's wife or mother, who knew what potential battle might be avoided? As for Queen Victoria, her problem was that she wanted every son, grandson, nephew, and great-nephew to be called Albert. There was an icy exchange between the waspish old Queen and her grandson, the future George v, on the naming of her great-grandson whom she ordered to be called Albert. The answer came back from the equally resolute father that the child was to be Edward in honour of his grandfather (later Edward VII). Victoria replied tartly that Edward's real name *was* Albert, but for once she did not get her own way. The child was given what must be, even by royal standards, the longest series of names in British history, Edward Albert Christian George Andrew Patrick David, and was ever afterwards known to the family as David. The Windsors have a habit of using familiar names other than the official one. David's (alias Edward VIII) younger brother George, later George VI, was always called Bertie. George v always called his mother, Queen Alexandra, 'Darling Mother Dear' and she in turn called him Georgie. Queen Victoria's eldest daughter Victoria, the Princess Royal, spent most of her childhood answering to Puss, Pussy, or even Pusette and it was not until much later that Vicky became her pet name. To this day Queen Elizabeth II is referred to as Lillibet by her closest friends and family. It is the name she grew up with when she couldn't pronounce Elizabeth. As for her granddaughter Miss Zara Phillips, when the family first heard the proposal to call Princess Anne's daughter by this unusual name, one of her horse-loving relatives murmured that it sounded more like the winner of the three-thirty at Lingfield.

As the christening service grew in pomp and importance, more

official dicta were laid down as to precisely how many duchesses should carry the train and how many belted earls should hover by the font. George III, who presided over more christenings than any other British monarch, took the occasions very seriously – and extravagantly for a man who was notoriously penny pinching in his own home; he made the children drink tea without sugar because sugar was so expensive. His third daughter's christening mantle was a fairy-tale garment twenty-two feet long, made of stiff white silk, lined with pale pink taffeta edged with ermine, the centre panel being thickly encrusted with jewels. The whole outfit set the Treasury back £2,800. At least the nation got its money's worth

The christening of Vicky, the Princess Royal, in 1841 in the Throne Room of Buckingham Palace. The ceremony was stage-managed by the Prince Consort (far right), but it was the Duke of Wellington (third from left), one of the Princess's godparents, who stole the show

The gold font in Buckingham Palace, which is now used for most royal christenings

for, by this time, the fashion for stripping the baby and all but drowning it had died out so that the little princess got as much wear as possible out of her christening dress.

George, with his brood of fifteen, was happy to treat his sons and daughters with equality when it came to christenings, birthdays, and anniversaries. He frankly preferred his daughters. Queen Victoria shamelessly preferred the boys in her family. She did not particularly show them more affection, but ensured that the boys always took, and were seen to take, precedence in public. We have already heard of the sumptuousness of her eldest son's christening. A very human and almost gossipy account of the occasion comes to us from a letter written by Sarah Spencer, Lady Lyttleton, one of the Queen's ladies-in-waiting. It was written soon afterwards to a female friend.

> When the Duchess of Buccleuch [one of the baby's sponsors] set off to do her arduous part taking the Prince of Wales and giving him up to and then taking him back from the Archbishop, she made a little room and I forced my way into it so as to see the child perfectly and also how well she did it, and how neatly she picked up his Royal Highness, mantle and lace and all, out of the voluminous folds of the Primate's lawn sleeves and the danger to his wig which, it was feared, the Prince might have lain hold of and brought away at least on quitting his arms. I did not even see what I had admired – the Queen's very devout and affecting manner of kneeling quite down, in spite of her cumbrous robes of the Garter, on first entering the church.

This genuflection was another example of the Queen's preference for princes, which she had first expressed minutes after the Princess Royal was born. She did not kneel on first entering the church at little Pusette's christening. The Princess Royal's christening had been something of a pantomime, stage managed by her father Albert. It was the Prince Consort who personally designed the christening cake which boasted on top of the highest tier a replica of Neptune, trident in hand, standing beside Britannia who, instead of a trident, was carrying a baby. Albert also wrote a special anthem for the occasion which was to be sung when the baby headed the long procession into the Throne Room of

84

Princess Elizabeth of Edinburgh holding her baby son, Prince Charles, after his christening at Buckingham Palace in December 1948. The infant Prince is wearing the traditional royal christening gown of Holland lace over Spitalfields silk

Buckingham Palace. Unfortunately for Albert the whole production was thrown out of gear by the late arrival of the Duke of Wellington for, as soon as he came in, the choir broke off singing the anthem and burst into a joyful rendering of 'See the Conquering Hero Comes'.

All Queen Victoria's children were, and every royal baby born in this country since has been, christened in the same gown. Fortunately twins do not seem to run in the royal strain. It is a garment fashioned in a fairy-tale, made of pure Holland lace over Spitalfields silk with petticoats almost as elaborately embroidered as the dress itself, and with enough frills to clothe a *corps de ballet* for *Swan Lake*. Whenever a new royal child is born the Queen, who is custodian of the robe, sends it round to the appropriate household where it will lie, as it did recently, on a bed in the night nursery of Barnwell or Kensington Palace and soon doubtless Highgrove, waiting for its new occupant. Over the years it has changed colour, from white to cream, from cream to ivory, from ivory to icy, smooth magnolia.

IV

Others
as Mothers

It is the summer of 1689. Amid national rejoicing and clarions from every parish church tower, the future Queen Anne has given birth to a son to be named William Duke of Gloucester. This is Anne's seventh pregnancy. So far she has had a still-born daughter, two sickly daughters who have not survived infancy, and three miscarriages. The child is pale and puny. If he were not royal he would certainly have been called a runt. Still, a fine, sturdy, young wet-nurse has been found for him in the shape of a Mrs Shermon at whose breast he appears to thrive. For six weeks the child waxes, his cheeks fill out, his belly swells, his delighted parents receive the usual crowd of well-wishers at Hampton Court, and then, quite suddenly, the little Duke begins to fail. He coughs, he cries, he loses weight. Doctors are summoned. They prod and they poke and they peer and, at last, they come up with the reason. The root, or possible roots, of the problem, they say, are Mrs Shermon's nipples. They are much too big. Poor little baby William cannot stretch his pretty rosebud mouth round those enormous crinkled peaks. Sobbing, Mrs Shermon is sent packing and a Mrs Wanley, who suckled the Queen's second living daughter Princess Anne Sophia, and who is now, like all the best milk bottles, conveniently waiting on the doorstep, is recalled to active service.

Eureka. The little lad rallies. Once more the roses bloom in his cheeks and he puts on weight. Mrs Wanley diligently rubs almond oil into her manageable, medium-sized nipples to keep them soft

and crack-proof, and whenever her charge shows any signs of
wind or gripes she drinks quantities of peppermint water and
lemon extract which will come out in her milk and cure his
discomfort. And then, inexplicably, after another six weeks the
child's sickness returns. He will not suck. He grows thin and
feverish. Worse, he begins to convulse, one attack coming so hard
upon the last that the distraught mother sends three separate
messengers post-haste to London for the physician. Down come
the doctors, leeches, enemas, and compounds at the ready. More
prodding. It is the milk, they say (this is beginning to be a familiar
refrain), His Royal Highness needs a change of milk. Now Mrs
Wanley is sent sobbing and sorrowing away and a large notice is
pinned to the railings of Hampton Court Palace in much the same
way as one might place a card in the newsagent's window asking
for a piano tuner or a chimney sweep, except that in this case their
royal highnesses are looking for a wet-nurse. Suitable candidates
are requested to come immediately to the Palace for auditions.

The news travels like a bush fire. Within hours of the notice
going up a stream of young hopefuls, many with their infants in
tow, descends on Hampton Court. It is not pure patriotism that

persuades them to the royal feet, it is the certain knowledge that they will probably earn enough money over the next two years to keep them in comfort for life. Royal wet-nurses have always been handsomely rewarded and, as long ago as 1413, Henry v on ascending the throne granted a pension of £20 a year (£5,000 by today's reckoning) on his former wet-nurse, Joanna Waring. And didn't Henry viii do the same for his, Mrs Anne Luke? Crowds of lactating ladies gather in the ante-room and queues stretch from the Palace to the river. Charlotte, Lady Beverwort, one of the Queen's Women of the Bedchamber, is appointed chief quality controller and weeder-out of unsuitable applicants. Many of the mothers lie about the age of their children in order to make their milk younger, but Lady Charlotte cunningly checks their children's birthdays in the parish register and those that have lied are booted out.

Valuable time is being lost. The little Prince is sinking. A score of wet-nurses who have passed the first interview and are waiting on the short list have been tried out on the poor, confused baby, but he still does not thrive. And then one day, passing through the ante-room on his way to visit his son, Prince George spots a large, robust, red-faced, and none too clean woman with a one-month-old child in her arms and the most enormous bosoms he has ever seen. Overwhelmed at the prospect of the nourishment within, the promise of pneumatic bliss, the Prince commands the woman, whose name is Pack, to follow him to his wife's bedchamber. Her foul appearance and malodorous condition revolt the sensitive waiting women, but the Prince waves away their protests and instructs Mrs Pack to lie down with the still convulsing infant and feed him. Doctors, nurses, nursemaids, footmen, stand at the foot of the bed and hold their breath. Mrs Pack unveils one of her magic mountains and offers it to the baby. He sucks. The convulsions stop and a great sigh of relief runs through the bystanders. Once again the Stuarts have a viable dynasty.

From that moment forth Mrs Pack's career can only be described as meteoric. Prince George gave orders that Mrs Pack was to have whatever she wanted to eat and drink whenever she wanted it. She was not to be opposed in any way. This was tough on the permanent household for Mrs Pack was a foul-mouthed, foul-tempered, foul-smelling harridan who rarely washed and never changed her clothes. And yet her unique position as the royal cow made her supreme. Her reign of terror continued when the household moved from Hampton Court to Craven House in Kensington. After Anne she was the most important member of the household. Beneath her she had two chief nurses, Mrs Atkinson and Mrs Fortress, who in turn had their own staff. Altogether there were thirty servants involved solely in the running of the nursery including cooks, seamstresses, footmen, valets, grooms, and nurserymaids. Fortunately for the tyrannized staff the Behemoth of the Bedchamber did not last for long. Those fine, ruddy cheeks that had first attracted Prince George to her, along with her breasts, were less the result of outdoor living as heavy drinking. With her new unlimited access to alcohol at the Palace her health started to fail and only a few months after the family moved to Kensington, Mrs Pack died. The Duke of Gloucester was by now holding his own, no new wet-nurse was employed, and Mrs Pack was buried with much rejoicing afterwards in the servants' hall.

There is only one Mrs Pack in this story of royal nurses, but though she was a grotesque caricature of the profession, many of her qualities apply in general. Until the middle of the nineteenth century babies of royal, noble, and gentle birth were, with few exceptions, handed over to wet-nurses immediately after birth. Often the child would be minded in the nurse's own home which further deprived it of direct contact with its natural mother. Wet-nurses were chosen with great care for it was widely held that morality came out with the milk. A sober, quiet, church-going girl was preferred, also if possible without red hair. Fiery hair made for fiery characters. In the eleventh century a law forbade Christian children to be suckled by Jewish wet-nurses and vice-versa. The reason for this is obscure though it was said that Jewish wet-nurses refused to feed their charges on the Sabbath. Queen Henrietta Maria, wife of Charles I, was at the heart of a furious argument because she saw fit to use a Catholic wet-nurse for the Protestant heir to the British throne. Petitions were made to the King pointing out the possible dangers of such an arrangement. The King, fed up with his wife's overcrowded household of four hundred expatriate French persons, including sixty Catholic priests, instructed his wife to change her dairymaid and dismiss most of her staff, neither of which instructions she heeded.

To increase the supply of milk in the breast a medieval recipe suggests a mixture containing the whites of raw eggs, oil of violets, a portion of plaster or pitch, pounded and mixed with the oil of roses, together with a goodish quantity of doves' dung and the dregs of wine or ale, the whole lot – thank heavens – not being eaten, but used more as a poultice to place against the breast to stimulate increase. Maybe Tudor wet-nurses with their bawdy good humour would have suffered this, but one can scarcely imagine Queen Victoria's pious band of nurses allowing such a heathen brew to be cooked up in the royal nursery.

There is a poem about the ideal wet-nurse, translated from the original sixteenth-century Latin by H.W. Tytler (appropriately enough) two hundred years later, part of which runs thus:

> *Choose one of middle age nor old nor young,*
> *Nor plump nor slim her make but firm and strong.*
> *Upon her cheek let health refulgent glow*
> *In vivid colours that good humour show.*
> *Long be her arms and broad her ample chest*
> *Her neck be finely turned and full her breast.*
> *Let the twin hills be white as mountain snow*
> *Their swelling veins with circling juices flow.*
> *Each in a well-projected nipple end*
> *And milk in copious streams from these descend . . .*
> *Remember too, the whitest milk you meet*
> *Of grateful flavour, pleasing taste and sweet.*

Royal wet-nurses were chosen with the utmost care and screening – character, breeding, disposition, habits, age, complexion were taken into consideration. A girl with a sluttish disposition or reputation as a coquette need not apply. Guillemeau, a sixteenth-century French doctor, wrote a pamphlet on the attributes that a good wet-nurse should possess. They read like the entry under 'perfection' in Roget's *Thesaurus*. Among other things, he says, a wet-nurse should be sober, even-tempered, wise, happy, chaste, discreet, well-born, careful, understanding, conscientious, and always willing to bare her bosom to her infant charge no matter when he should demand it. (Demand feeding was always practised. It is only in the regimental atmosphere of twentieth-century hospitals that mothers have been bludgeoned into feeding their offspring at set times.) A couple of hundred years after Guillemeau's pronouncements on the perfect mobile dairy, the eminent French obstetrician Mauriceau, who put the famous Chamberlen forceps to the acid test, hardened up the prejudice against red-heads with more scientifically based proof. The breast milk of red-haired women, he wrote in a medical journal, had a sour, stinking and bad scent.

Another school of thought in the sixteenth century held that the best wet-nurses were aged between twenty-five and thirty-five and should recently have been delivered of a large, male child. Exercise was essential for these nurses, especially exercises that made use of the muscles of the upper torso, such as weaving or grinding or spinning. For some inexplicable reason Irish women were not thought to be suited to this calling, possibly because of their red hair, but probably because some of their methods of rearing children were unconventional if not downright barbaric. The Irish used a curious medieval device like a pendulous satchel made of leather with a slit at one side. This was hung on some convenient hook and the baby placed inside with just its eyes peeping out of the gap. An infant Earl of Cork was left hanging in one of these weird devices by an absent-minded nurse for the entire night.

The simplest and the most traditional way of testing to see if a wet-nurse's milk was any good was the Nail Test. This is similar to the housewife's method of testing to see if homemade marmalade has set. The Nail Test came down from Roman times and was still being used at the end of the nineteenth century. A drop of breast milk was placed on the middle of a fingernail with the hand placed flat on the table. The finger was then tilted slightly allowing the milk to drip off the end of the nail. If it did not drip but clung stickily and sluggishly to the nail it was too thick. If it gushed over the edge it was too thin. The best quality milk was just thick enough to drop slowly from the side of the nail.

But what if, after all these precautions, the child would not feed? The fretful wet-nurse's first apprehensive thoughts would turn to that old superstition about changeling children, for it was buried deep in folklore that a child who would not take nourishment was surely a fairy child. It was equally well remembered by these superstitious crones that a changeling child could drink its nurse dry 'but profiteth not. Its belly doth not thrive.' One device to encourage an indifferent feeder was the milking horn, exactly what its name suggests. This was a short piece of cow's horn with a hole at one end through which the milk flowed, either slowly or quickly depending on the amount of cloth wedged into the horn. The first mention of a feeding-bottle as such in this country was in the early seventeenth century when a certain Master Marmaduke Rawden was fed through an ingenious sucking bottle by his nurse because he had burned his mouth so badly while playing with fireworks. Another old wives' remedy was to rub a reluctant child's gums with aloes so that he would develop a rare thirst. There was also a variety of pap boats and tiny spoons for feeding children. Pap was bread mixed with milk and panada was the name for cereal boiled to a pulp in broth. A fine collection of royal feeding-bottles is on display at the Victoria and Albert Museum in South Kensington, including some beautifully worked silver pap boats that belonged to Charles I.

This was undoubtedly a cleaner way to feed a child than the usual method (not – thank heavens – practised on delicate royal babies) where the wet-nurse chewed the bread to a lumpfree pulp in her mouth, damped it down with a drop or two of milk squeezed by hand from her bosom and then fed it to the child on the end of her finger. Hygiene did not play a significant part in this exercise, which could not have improved the infant mortality level. Another popular, but somewhat exclusive, remedy for encouraging a stubborn child to feed was to hold it up to the teat of an ass. Ass's milk was actually prescribed by physicians in French hospitals before the Revolution and the little Dauphin who was to become Louis XIII was himself held up by his nurse to drink from such a beast.

Queen Charlotte's problem was not her wet-nurses' milk, but their manners. She was forever having rows with her nurses, the chief offender being Mrs Margaret Scott who came to the Queen as a wet-nurse having just borne her twelfth child. Although Mrs Scott was almost as fecund a mother as the sovereign, she was a bit too grand to take a sufficiently subservient place in the royal nursery. Her family was distantly related to the Buccleuchs and, though she nursed the infant Prince Regent with devotion and success and stayed on a year or two after he had been weaned to help with the other children, she was far too autocratic for the easy-going Queen. Thereafter, Charlotte made a point of employing less well-connected wet-nurses. Both the Dukes of

Mother Iak.

Mistress Jak, Edward VI's wet-nurse, from a drawing by Holbein

York and Kent were fed by vicars' wives. The Duke of Kent's Mrs Percy was a particularly cheerful soul whose husband later became a bishop – another occupational perk no doubt.

It was a tradition beginning with Henry v that Princes of Wales should be farmed out to Welsh wet-nurses, for in this way it would be guaranteed that the child's first spoken words would be in Welsh, a fitting and auspicious sign of future good fortune. Madcap Harry was born at Monmouth, but being a weak and puny child he was immediately despatched to Cornfield, some six miles away, to the waiting arms and dugs of that fine Welsh lass Joanna Waring of whom he became so fond and whom he rewarded so handsomely in later life. Some mementoes of Harry's stay with Joanna still survive and give an endearing picture of his infancy. The wardrobe accounts record a payment for a long gown for the Lord Henry. And later, in early boyhood, there is note of an invoice for eight pence for the Prince's harp strings, and a further four shillings for seven grammar books which sounds a little pricey for the period. Joanna called him her 'fond cockering' and spoiled him shamelessly, for she stayed with him long after he had been weaned.

Wet-nurses were steeped in traditional wisdom and common sense mixed with the spells and nonsense of folklore. Premature babies who had to make up ground rapidly were encouraged to feed more often by a variation of the aloes-on-the-gums method. Salt was rubbed under their fingernails when they were put to bed and the child, as usual, fell asleep sucking its fingers. This would, of course, make it thirsty and therefore wake more frequently than a full-term baby. George II's children's Hertfordshire wet-nurse, the wife of one of the royal gardeners, practised this little trick on her eight-week premature charge and brought him to lusty good health by the time he was six months. King John's wet-nurse, Agatha, a West Country woman, had a cure for toothache which could have come straight out of a horror film. This involved burning a candle made of mutton fat mixed with the crushed seeds of the plant sea holly. The lighted candle was then held up close to the affected tooth and a bowl of water placed underneath. The idea was that the worm gnawing inside the tooth, and undoubtedly the cause of the toothache, would feel the heat of the candle and emerge, whereupon, said Agatha knowingly, it would fall into the water and drown. It was an imaginative remedy.

95

Maybe it was used on the young Elizabeth Tudor who suffered horribly as a child from toothache. Lady Bryan who had charge of the future Queen wrote in a letter to a friend

> God knoweth My Lady hath great pain with her great teeth and they come very slowly forth which causeth me to suffer Her Grace to have her will more than I would. I trust to get her teeth well graft and to have her Grace after another fashion than she is yet, so as I trust the King's grace shall have great comfort in her grace. For she is as toward a child and as gentle of conditions as I ever knew any in my life.

Another favourite wet-nurse cure was for constipation. Fly dung mixed with poppy seeds was the wonder drug and, because this coarse mixture was almost impossible to administer to a small baby, the devoted wet-nurse would consent to swallow the stuff herself and hope that the effect would be brought out in the milk at the next feed.

With few exceptions children of royal, noble and gentle birth began their lives in the laps of wet-nurses. The fashion changed only during the last century when some eminent Victorian doctors published pamphlets exhorting mothers to feed their own children. Like everything else connected with child care the fashion for breast-feeding comes and goes. It is very much in vogue at the moment. The usual practice for royal mothers these days is to feed their children for around three months and then put them onto one of the many commerical dried baby milk products on the market. With the crammed social and working schedule that our princesses have to observe, for they are all very active in and conscientious about their public duties, the luxury of feeding their own babies for more than a few months is impracticable. Only three months after the birth of Lord Frederick Windsor his mother Princess Michael of Kent was back at work with the interior decorating business she runs from her office in Kensington Palace. While she was out at work giving estimates for the redecoration of the Saudi Arabian Embassy, her young Scottish nanny Jean (who graduated *victor ludorum* from the Norland Nursery nursing academy in Berkshire) was busily washing out feeding-bottles in the nursery kitchen. The Danish-born Duchess of Gloucester has also fed all three of her children, Alexander, Davina, and baby

Towards the end of the eighteenth century, the practice of giving babies to wet-nurses gradually declined and it became fashionable for high-class mothers to breast-feed their children. This satirical print, published the year of Princess Charlotte's birth, illustrates the new vogue

Rose, returning to the seclusion of her country home in Barnwell for the three months after their births. Here she refrained from all public duties until they had all acquired mature immunity from at least a twelve-week period of mother's milk.

Standing on the side of the sink in the second-floor nursery of Gatcombe Park in Gloucestershire, the home of Princess Anne and Captain Mark Phillips, is one of those large sterilizing tanks available in most baby shops which hold six plastic feeding-bottles. Princess Anne breast-fed both her children, Peter and Zara, for the first three months after which the nanny took over with the bottled variety. To assist her while she was breast-feeding the Princess wore one of the special maternity brassières designed by the National Childbirth Trust. They are very plain and sturdy, made of cotton, and fasten at the front with hooks and with long laces at the back to ensure a comfortable fit.

There are exceptional examples of royal mothers feeding their babies before Victorian times. The Black Prince was fed at his own mother's breast which, it was said, accounted for his prowess on the battlefield. And there were also a couple of French royals who flouted convention, by eschewing substitute milk. A Queen Blanche of Castile stuck her fingers down the throat of her baby son to make him vomit when she learned that in her absence the child had been given a little snack by a passing wet-nurse. And as for the highly educated Countess Ida of Boulogne, she all but took leave of her senses when she found that one of her three sons had been handed to a deputy for nourishment while she was at Mass. Countess Ida had left her three little treasures, Eustace, Godfrey, and Baldwin, in the care of a young nursemaid who was not aware of her mistress's revulsion for wet-nursing. When one of the little chaps woke up whimpering, with the best will in the world she handed him over to a wet-nurse. The Countess returned and was informed of the incident. She at once flew into a desperate passion. A contemporary account continues thus:

> Her heart shook, she fell back in her seat, she gasped, she called herself a poor leper. Swiftly, she flew all trembling with rage and caught the child under the arms, the child of tender flesh she caught him in her hands. Her face was as black as the coal with the wrath that seized within. There on a mighty table she bade them spread out a purple quilt and hold the child. Then she rolled him and caught him by the shoulders that he delayed not to give up the milk which he had sucked.

The wretched nursemaid fled from her mistress's presence, 'more benumbed than worm in wintertime'.

So far three women have played major roles in the little prince's life: his mother, who bore him and then virtually abandoned him to her surrogate while she regained her strength, prepared herself for the churching and christening ceremonies, and, as like as not, became pregnant again – she did not, of course, benefit from the natural contraceptive qualities of lactation; the midwife, who delivered him (charging high for the service if he were a boy and lower if only a girl), cut the cord with a small silver blade, and then carefully counted the wrinkles inside his navel to see how potent he would be (no wrinkles, no dice); and, finally, the wet-nurse. But now the baby is ready to be weaned – at around eighteen months for a girl, two years for a boy. The usual method of weaning was to rub mustard over the nipples to discourage the child from sucking. And now we meet the most important person in the life of the royal child until he has reached puberty. Enter the nanny.

Nannies in royal households played a curiously complex role: part-servant, part-tyrant, part-confidante. There were strict nannies and soft nannies, martinets and marshmallows. Both Elizabeth Tudor and Elizabeth Windsor were fortunate in having devoted attendants who, as the children grew into adulthood, remained intimate friends. Lady Bryan, who was appointed governor or guardian to the first Elizabeth when she was three years old, was ever prepared to stand up for her infant mistress's rights. Time and again she stuck her neck out to get recognition for Elizabeth (and heaven knows, sticking your neck out in Tudor times when the executioner's block loomed large was a dangerous attitude). She was particularly supportive after the birth of Prince Edward when Elizabeth was abandoned by her father who was besotted with his new son and heir. She was not the first of his children to be snubbed. Poor Princess Mary had been demoted when she herself was born, stripped of the title of Princess of Wales and compelled to suffer the further humiliation of being Elizabeth's lady-in-waiting. Now it was Elizabeth's turn to suffer. Her mother Anne Boleyn had been disgraced, denounced, and finally decapitated and Elizabeth might well have been deprived of any birth rights were it not, ironically, for the solicitude of her new soft-hearted step-mother, Jane Seymour. Elizabeth had been sent to the country to Hunsdon with Lady Bryan to mind her. Henry neglected the Hunsdon household shamelessly. There were few attendants and no luxuries. There don't seem to have been many clothes either. In a letter of supplication to the King, Lady Bryan wrote: 'She [Elizabeth] hath neither gown, nor kirtle nor petticoat, nor no manner of linen, nor foresmocks, nor kerchiefs, nor rails, nor body stichets, nor handkerchiefs, nor

Left: *Princess Elizabeth in 1928 with her nanny, Mrs Clara Knight*

Right: *Princess Elizabeth taking her first tentative steps in the playground behind her Piccadilly home under the eagle eye of her nurse*

sleeves nor mufflers nor biggins.' Doubtless the deprived little Princess could have existed without body stichets or corsets or even the foresmocks or aprons, but biggin (or bonnet) and no dress must have been a tiresome deprivation.

There was no shortage of biggins at 11 Bruton Street, Mayfair, where the second Queen Elizabeth spent the first two years of her life. Mrs Clara Knight was her nanny. She was a sort of hand-me-down family retainer, first employed twenty years earlier by the family as a nanny to Elizabeth Bowes-Lyon. Mrs Knight and an under-nurse had their work cut out servicing the little Princess's huge wardrobe, which included at least a hundred bonnets. One of the earliest pictures of the baby Princess showed her wearing a lacy layette, jacket and bonnet, in primrose yellow. Overnight the pink-for-a-girl syndrome was out and primrose yellow in. Mrs

Knight, nicknamed Alla since none of her babies had been able to get their tiny tongues round Clara, loved dressing and undressing Lillibet. Her entire ensemble was changed twice a day (laundry costs being no object in those days of full employment) and some-times more if Grandfather was paying a call. Mrs Knight was assisted in her work by an under-nanny, Margaret Macdonald, code-named Bobo. It was Bobo who helped the two-year-old Princess groom, saddle, and bridle the large collection of toy horses she tethered every night outside her bedroom door. Mrs Knight was an old-fashioned family retainer who never took holidays or days off and had firm views about flapjacks and rice pudding. Bobo, who was just twenty-two when the Princess was born, was a jollier companion and when Margaret Rose arrived five years later, demanding Mrs Knight's undivided attention,

Katherine of France, Henry V's Queen, in childbed at Windsor in 1421. Her nurserymaids are carrying the swaddled infant Prince – the future Henry VI

Bobo and Princess Elizabeth became great chums. She was to become one of the Queen's most intimate friends, officially her dresser, but really more a companion and confidante who went with her on all her tours. Bobo invariably featured in those pictures of the Queen descending aircraft steps as one of the small gaggle of anonymous attendants bringing up the rear.

But we are jumping the gun. A royal nanny's duties in bygone days were infinitely more diverse than merely worrying about the biggin count. Every single aspect of the child's welfare, apart from the early feeding which was done by the wet-nurse, was in their hands. The earliest royal nannies had a relatively cushy life because swaddling took the strain out of babycare. A swaddled baby was by definition a docile baby. Incarcerated in all those bandages, it could hardly be otherwise. Swaddled babies slept most of the time and what was even more convenient, if the cradle was not at hand, they could be hung on a hook by the fire while the nanny got on with the washing. For light relief the nursemaids might pass away an idle hour by tossing the swaddled baby (which was almost the same size and shape as a rugger ball) into the air or to each other in a merry game of handball. Not quite so merry in the case of one of the younger brothers of the French King, Henri IV. He was being tossed back and forth over a windowsill in the upper-floor nursery by two nursemaids when, by accident, one of the players dropped the ball. The child fell out of the window, bashing his head on the stone pavings, and broke his little neck. A bad case of butterfingers.

Once unswaddled at about eighteen months, at the same time as he was being weaned from the breast, the child would then be taught by his nurse how to walk. Crawling was not allowed. Children were not animals, went the argument, and therefore they should walk upright from the start. An ingenious collection of baby-walking gadgets was devised. The wooden walking frame on wheels was fitted under the child's armpits to keep it vertical. Then there were the leading strings or reins which would be tied onto the child's arms and legs and head so that he could be manipulated like a puppet by his minder. Royal children had lavishly embroidered leading reins. Museum visitors in Scotland can see the richly ornamented pair stitched by Mary Queen of Scots during her pregnancy for baby James. Tudor and Stuart nurseries also used a wonderfully practical device for protecting the fragile heads of future monarchs called 'black puddings'. These were large, thickly padded hats made of black velvet which were tied firmly onto the head with ribbons and acted as a crash helmet. The only problem was their weight, especially if some well-meaning nanny had sewn on a few jewels to make the whole thing more regal. A less appealing device was the horrifying metal cage in which some Victorian nannies locked their charges into bed at night to keep their arms away from their bodies and so stop the children masturbating.

Nannies were full of nursery lore handed down over the centuries. If, for instance, a child was to rise to a higher station in life its first movement must be upwards. This was an essential move for second sons. The simplest way would be for the nurse to carry the child upstairs, but if, as often happened, the nursery was on the

Anthony van Dyck's painting of five of the children of Charles I and Henrietta Maria, painted in 1637. The children are, left to right, Mary who married the Prince of Orange, James, Duke of York, Charles, Prince of Wales, Elizabeth and Anne. The younger children are dressed in exactly the same way, regardless of sex

top floor of the house, a superstitious nurse would step up onto a chair which had the same elevating effect. Pull a baby through a cleft in a straight-trunked tree and it would not get rickets. Coral, as already stated, was lucky, so a coral rattle was one of the child's earliest playthings. But coral was expensive and poorer homes that couldn't afford it used animal bladders filled with dried peas which rattled just as noisily. The early nurses were required to know all about medical cures too and, instead of the handy all-in-one first aid box in the bathroom cupboard of modern homes, virtually all their patent medicines came from the herb garden. Every part of the child's body, according to the nanny, was associated with, and could be treated by, a different plant or herb. If a child, for example, had any sort of pain in its head – ear-ache, a stiff neck, eye strain, a blocked nose – then the nurse would bustle off into the knot garden and snip off a few sprigs of lavender or eyebright or sage or aniseed which she would then cook up in some clever way and apply either internally or as a sort of poultice over the affected spot. A child with a weak heart, the sickly little Edward II for one, could be fortified with compounds of borage, saffron, and basil. If a child caught a cold and had congested lungs, comfrey was prescribed. Comfrey was also the answer to rheumatic fever, a complaint suffered more by the nanny than her charge. And roses were good for everything, probably because of their scent which would take the patient's mind off his ailments. By the seventeenth century the nurse was losing out in medical expertise to the qualified physician, although some of their remedies were decidedly cranky. Charles II's physician, Dr King, had great faith in a patent medicine of the time that was supposed to be good for children's colic. Unfortunately, there were no legitimate children in Charles's nursery on which to try it, but no doubt the little bastards were given their daily dose of Daffy's Elixir which was made of caraway, aniseed, jalap, senna, and crushed juniper berries marinated for several days in alcohol and water and finally mixed to a sweet liquor with black treacle.

But surrounded by nannies, nurses, and physicians, Mother still very often knew best in noble households. Queen Charlotte swore by peppermint tea laced with a few drops of brandy as a cure-all for baby colic. Lady Althorp, now Mrs Shand Kydd, mother of the present Princess of Wales, was once so desperate to relieve her youngest daughter who was crying pitifully during a particularly bad bout of teething that she rummaged in her hand-bag for something, *anything*, for the fretful baby to bite on and came up with the small silver case in which she carried visiting cards. It worked like a charm. Diana bit hard on the case leaving dents in the lid with her infant teeth, but this was a small price to pay. Thereafter, Diana and the card case were inseparable, at least until all her teeth had come through.

Two separate and distinct schools of thought prevail in today's royal nurseries as to how to choose a suitable nanny for the new blue-blooded generation. The *nouvelles royales* – Austrian-born Princess Michael and Danish-born Princess Richard – plump for the *nouveau* type of nanny who has been college trained, has acquired everything she knows about child psychology from books, and demands a large salary with substantial time off and holidays. She may even belong to a trade union. Diametrically opposed to this view are the traditionalists like the Queen and Princess Alexandra, who wouldn't give twopence for any amount of NNEBs after a girl's name, but are interested only in someone with a pleasing personality who gets on with children.

Standing out like a beacon among history's hotchpotch of royal nannies is Nanny Anderson, 'our Mabel'. A Hollywood producer looking for the perfect stereotype Mary Poppins need look no further than this paragon of the playroom, who has been a member of the royal household for the last thirty-two years and has minded two generations of royal children (five altogether) and is even now poised to take charge of her sixth. At present Mabel Anderson is employed by the Prince and Princess of Wales as housekeeper in their Gloucestershire home of Highgrove, but doubtless Nanny Anderson will soon once again be chief bottle-washer in the nursery.

After the completely unexpected and cruel betrayal of the Royal Family's trust by Marion Crawford, the infamous Crawfie who converted her twelve years as governess to the little Princesses Elizabeth and Margaret Rose into royalties on all her literary *exposés*, the young Princess Elizabeth must have been a little apprehensive about choosing a nanny for her own baby son, Charles. Mabel Anderson was twenty-two, the same age as the Princess, when she went for that fateful interview at Buckingham Palace. She was a policeman's daughter, born in Bootle in Lancashire, educated at the local grammar school, with a passionate interest in children. She was the best babysitter in town. She had returned to her mother's old home in Elgin, forty miles from Balmoral, when her father was killed in the Merseyside Blitz. She had gone on to technical college to take a two-year course in domestic science, but the quiet, soft-voiced girl always knew where her real interest lay. She wanted to look after children.

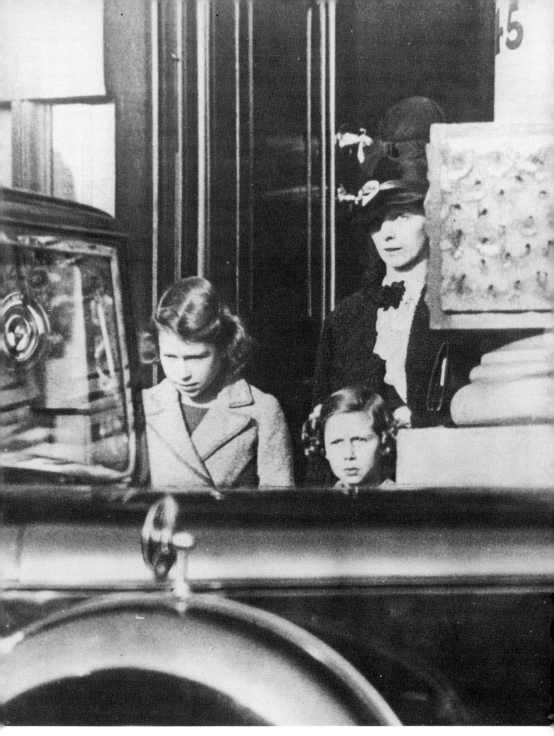

Princess Elizabeth and Princess Margaret Rose with their nanny, Marion Crawford, leaving 145 Piccadilly in 1936

Princess Elizabeth of Edinburgh, holding Prince Charles's hand, with Mabel Anderson, carrying Princess Anne

Her first job was with a South African family living in Scotland who had two small boys. She was a huge success. On rainy days she would take them off to the kitchen to make gingerbread men and, when the family left to go home to Johannesburg, Mabel, with a glowing reference, put her name down with the local employment exchange. She also advertised for a position in the *Lady* magazine, bastion of genteel respectability. Ever since Queen Victoria the royals have had a preference for Scottish nannies and the young Princess Elizabeth was no exception; Mabel was invited for an interview first at St James's and then at Buckingham Palace. The Princess was immediately taken with her quiet, unassuming but firm manner, her steady gaze, her unflappability. She was offered the job of under-nanny to Nurse Lightbody.

Mabel's talents lay chiefly in her instant sympathy with children. She never shouted at them or smacked them, but they always

Mabel Anderson taking Prince Edward, aged seven, to school in Kensington

obeyed and respected her. She could be firm, but she could also be fun. Charles and Anne adored her. She taught them to play hopscotch on the terrace, she let them paint their faces like Red Indians, she helped them press wild flowers from Windsor Great Park in the pages of telephone directories, she stuck their baby pictures of lopsided houses and legless animals up in the day nursery like a frieze. And, best of all, she told them magical stories about monsters and dragons and fairies and witches and, of course, horses. When Prince Charles published his own children's story a few years ago he said he owed the technique of telling good yarns to his nanny. Mabel was always brimming over with good ideas. She invented clever counting games for instance. The nursery at Buckingham Palace is in the north-east corner overlooking the Mall, and Mabel would lift Charles up to the window and make him count the black taxis or the horses or how many strides the scarlet-coated soldier on sentry duty took every

109

time he marched from his box to the railings and back. In those days you could actually see the sentries because they marched *outside* the railings. And with Princess Anne, her favourite charge as she later admitted, she invented a wonderful new form of hide and seek, a variation on the traditional game. Mabel taught the royal corgis to do the hiding while she and Anne waited indoors. She would give a command and the dogs would race off and hide in the bushes or behind the trees in the Palace gardens, and then Mabel and Anne would go seek.

Mabel had a flat on the second floor of Buckingham Palace, but practically no private life. She never had a boyfriend like other girls at her age. Her job was her entire life. When Prince Charles and Princess Anne were both past the age of needing a nanny, Mabel felt she should move on to another family. Royal nannies were often passed from one branch of the family to another (Mrs Knight, who had looked after Queen Elizabeth the Queen Mother and the Queen as children, went on to the Gloucesters). And then, to everyone's delight, not least of all Mabel's, ten years after Princess Anne's birth the Queen announced that she was expecting her third child. Mabel and her gingerbread men were back in business.

If possible, she was even more devoted to the Queen's 'second' family, Andrew and Edward, than she had been to Charles and Anne. After Andrew was born she did not take a day off work from her duties for five months. So closely did she guard her treasures that when the Queen and Prince Philip went to Windsor at weekends they left baby Andrew at Buckingham Palace with Mabel rather than disturb his, or Mabel's, routine. It was the same with Edward. One Christmas, when Edward was just seven years old, he was rushed to Great Ormond Street with suspected appendicitis and Mabel and a large red Christmas stocking moved into the room next to his at the hospital.

The same arrangement pertained at the Palace. She always slept within earshot of the children and, if they woke in the night howling because of a nightmare or because their bedclothes had fallen off or because they had ear-ache, it was Mabel who comforted them, tucked them back into bed, and made them cups of cocoa. It was Mabel who replaced the chewed elastic on Princess Anne's school hat, who sewed royal blue Cash's name tapes on all their socks, told the Queen when Andrew needed new shoes or

Edward a new vest. When Anne married and left home she did not forget her old nanny and, whenever she came up to London from Camberley or Gatcombe, she would drop in to Mabel's flat for a cup of tea and a chat. When Princess Anne received the freedom of the City of London at a ceremony at the Guildhall, she especially requested that Mabel should be among the VIPs to see her.

And so it was natural that when Anne was expecting her first baby, Mabel, who had lately taken on more of a position as Lady-in-Waiting, should be the nanny to her favourite child's own son. For three years she ruled the roost in the apple green and white Gatcombe Park nursery. She was as fiercely loyal to Princess Anne as she had been to the Queen. Wild horses wouldn't drag any information from her about her employers, no matter how she was pestered by the press. As usual, she was polite, but firm. She had nothing to say. When the usual crowd of reporters gathered round the converted Scout hut in the tiny Gloucestershire village of Minchinhampton near Gatcombe to see three-year-old Peter arrive for his first day at nursery school, one hawk-eyed hack noticed a slight bump on Master Peter's head. 'How had it happened?' Nanny Anderson was asked. Clutching the little lad firmly by the hand she said 'No comment', and it was left to one of the royal bodyguards to reveal to the reporters that Peter had fallen off his bicycle in the garden.

Two months before Princess Anne's second child, Zara Anne Elizabeth, was due, Mabel Anderson left Gatcombe. The official reason, given by the Palace, was that she felt at fifty-five she was getting too old to look after babies and the job should go to a younger woman. The whispered story goes that Mistress and Nanny were not seeing eye to eye about bringing up baby and that Mabel, in her old age, had become too autocratic and inflexible. The popular press had stories of a blazing row between Anne and Nanny Anderson, but since Miss Anderson herself was 'holidaying indefinitely abroad' when the story broke, her version was not available for print. Not that she would have given anything away if she had been around. 'Abroad' in this case was back at her home in Scotland where she did the only thing she could honestly call a spare-time interest unconnected with her nannying. She played golf. The story does have a happy ending. Mabel was not thrown out on to the street, *Spock* in one hand, golf clubs in the other. Scarcely had the news of her departure from

Gatcombe leaked out than an offer of employment came from a close neighbour in the county, namely the Princess of Wales. She invited Miss Anderson to come immediately and get her new home into ship-shape working order. So Mabel became housekeeper at Highgrove, a position to which nannies are often elevated in their later years, where she has a pretty self-contained flat on the second floor and a bedroom overlooking the rose garden.

Mabel Anderson is one of the old school of Great British Nannies. Thirty years in the royal household and the privilege of writing RVO after her name haven't changed her. She doesn't show her age. Maybe the nursery at Buckingham Palace has some secret Shangri-la elixir in its bathroom cabinet mixed in with the Haliborange and milk of magnesia. She still favours classic tweed suits in muted colours, comfortable brogues, a good plain watch on which you can see at forty paces if it's time for high tea, and a large roomy handbag which can easily accommodate a bottle of cough linctus, a spare pair of socks or a teddy bear. With all the fuss and embarrassment caused to the Royal Family by disaffected staff turning super-grass and selling their stories of 'How I Butled for the Queen' to the popular magazines, every new member of the royal household has to promise in writing that they will not disclose the details of their employers' private lives. The idea of Nanny Anderson being asked to sign such an agreement would be unthinkable. Mabel would no more dream of giving anything away than she would dream of letting one of her children go to bed in his vest. Fortunately this oath-taking is a formality on the whole, for the present Royal Family has the happy knack of imbuing their staff with a natural loyalty. One of Prince Andrew's junior nursemaids, whose family works on the royal estate at Sandringham, and is now married to an art dealer in Chiswick, says she is constantly being quizzed by curious friends about her time with the Royal Family. Why is it, she wailed, that everyone wants to know whether Andrew liked Rice Crispies better than Sugar Puffs? Actually he didn't like either. All the royal children have been brought up on good Scottish porridge.

It is easy to see why the royals – most of them anyway – avoid the limelight. Publicity is not merely distasteful, it can also be dangerous. It cannot be an easy thing at this particular point in British history to have one's elder son receive the title of Earl of

112

Ulster. His mother, Princess Richard, Duchess of Gloucester, once confided to a friend that she wanted her son's existence to be forgotten until he was old enough to look after himself. In the Middle Ages royal children were sometimes used as hostages. With the prevailing political climate similarly ghastly conditions could apply today. Pity the poor royal mother in this respect at least.

As the formality and protocol steadily trickle out of royal life-styles, with princes going to ordinary preparatory schools and princesses racing off to Girl Guide camp, so the importance of the nanny also declines. A generation ago Prince Andrew, like his mother, was put into clean clothes twice a day to be presented to his parents, and the sort of clothes made of pure cotton that needed scrupulous ironing or pure wool that required careful handwashing. Over at Gatcombe, the young Anne Wallace, who was handed Zara in the back of the blue Rover car the minute Princess Anne left hospital, has a far more relaxed routine. Baby Zara leaves her doll's pram on the stairs, her bricks in the hall, her fluffy animal toys in the drawing-room. She does not have to be formally presented to her mother, for whenever the Princess is at home she is invariably playing up in the nursery with her children. Zara wears bright, practical, tough dungarees that can be put through the washing machine and scarcely need ironing.

Even at Kensington Palace, home of Princess Michael of Kent who is a stickler for protocol, the nursery is a haven of childish pleasures. Jean, Princess Michael's sturdy Scottish nanny, saves up stale bread in a paper bag, hustles Lord Frederick, aged three, into his red wellingtons, and takes him off to feed the ducks on the Serpentine. And if Prince Michael is at home, he comes too, like any other proud father. Mrs Bill would not have approved at all of this casual approach. Mrs Bill was the devoted protector of the baby George VI or Bertie. She did not hold with new-fangled ways of allowing children to eat what they pleased and make too much noise, but Bertie adored her. When he went off to Dartmouth to train as a naval cadet he was mercilessly teased because of his stutter and his sticking out ears. And it was to Mrs Bill that he came running in the holidays, in Mrs Bill's large white apron that he buried his face, and to her he confided that the other cadets called him Bat Lugs and pricked him with pins to see if he really had blue blood. King George and Queen Mary, though kindly,

113

were not warm parents and it was left to Mrs Bill to give him the affection he needed. Heaven help any bully who dared to call one of Nanny Anderson's children Bat Lugs. Scottish nannies are not to be taken lightly.

V

Reading, Writing and Ruling

If blue blood and brains were natural bed-fellows, the story of the education of the forty-two monarchs who have occupied the British throne since the Norman Conquest would be an easier one to tell. Their intellectual abilities, however, are as varied as any that a teacher facing an unstreamed class of forty-two children might expect to find. There have been wise kings, lunatic kings, brilliant kings, and inept kings. To some extent tutors have influenced their characters. How significant this influence has been is best described in the words of Lord Melbourne, speaking to Queen Victoria, 'Be not over solicitous about education. It may be able to do much . . . it may mould and direct character, but it rarely changes it.'

The chances are that the Prince Regent would still have turned into the hard-drinking, hell-raising *roué* that he eventually became if he had been reared in a Trappist monastery but, given the weak, ineffectual, and terrified tutors appointed to teach him and his young brother, the Duke of York, the decline was precipitated. They drank openly in the schoolroom. By the time he was sixteen, Frederick Duke of York (the Grand Old Duke of the nursery rhyme) could put away six bottles of claret before his dinner without turning a hair. And Edward ii, on whom every attention had been lavished in the form of tutors, governors, and guardians, was so hopeless at classics that one of his mother's French relatives

115

remarked that he was little better than a crowned ass. It would be convenient, but inaccurate, to claim that the education of princes corresponds to contemporary academic attitudes. The Tudors may prove this rule, but then the Tudor schoolroom was unique; some of the better-educated exceptions to it grew up in the turbulent Middle Ages, while the twentieth century, with its democratic leaning towards higher education for everyone, has produced no high fliers in academic circles. It is true that Prince Charles managed a second-class degree in archaeology and anthropology at Trinity College, Cambridge, and Prince Richard, Duke of Gloucester, is a qualified architect, but no one could pretend that either of them is an intellectual. By far the cleverest of royal children were those three little Tudors, Princess Elizabeth, Prince Edward her half-brother, and their cousin Lady Jane Grey. Put any of them in a sixth form today and they would be called scholarship material. They were lucky to be coming up for school age at the same time as the first over-powering surge of Renaissance enthusiasm was sweeping into the country from Italy. Never had learning simply for its own sake been so prized and the phenomenal academic achievements reached by this Tudor trio, and to a lesser extent by the schoolboy James I, makes the academic records of the princes and princesses who followed them seem small beer.

Seventeen-year-old Princess Anne came away from her hearty, horsy boarding school with unspectacular 'O' and 'A' levels and a certain dexterity with a lacrosse stick. Before they had celebrated their ninth birthdays, Lady Jane Grey and Elizabeth Tudor had reached what would now be 'A' level standard in classics, the humanities, and modern languages. If we are looking for a nutshell description of royal education in the last thousand years it goes something like this: medieval princes were taught to be soldiers and statesmen; Renaissance princes dispensed with practical soldiering (do not be fooled by all those ornamental suits of armour behind glass cases in the Tower of London purporting to have belonged to Henry VIII: most of them were indeed ornamental or intended for the tiltyard) and added scholarship to the curriculum; Hanoverian princes abandoned scholarship, substituted sophistication, and re-introduced military prowess; twentieth-century royal education attempts, and largely succeeds, in combining the lot, scholar, statesman, soldier, and, in

116

Elizabeth Tudor, painted in 1546 when she was thirteen. The painter has chosen to portray the young Princess with her books – entirely apt, as she was an outstanding classical scholar

some respects, glass of fashion and mould of form as well. Not for nothing has Prince-of-Wales check become a perennial fashion favourite. As princes go, Prince Charles has gone to great lengths to get a broad education, from the freezing, bare-knees, and cold-baths atmosphere of Gordonstoun, near Inverness, to the blazing heat of Geelong Grammar School in Australia with stints at Cambridge, Aberystwyth, Dartmouth, and Chatham.

But to begin at the beginning. Until the Tudors moved into Westminster, bringing the divided country to a much needed period of peaceful coexistence, the main preoccupation of little princes lay not so much in keeping facts in their young heads as in keeping their young heads upon their young shoulders. The four hundred years between William the Conqueror and Henry VII were tempestuous. From their earliest childhood the Norman kings were taught the art of war. William's first mouthful of solid food was handed to him on the point of a sword, and he grew up to be more adept at handling a sword than a pen. The three Rs stood for riding, routing, and ransacking with extra-curricular activities such as skirmishing, laying siege, laying waste, escaping from dungeons, storming castles, and sundry other martial skills. Bearing this in mind it is hardly surprising that William the Conqueror was illiterate, as was William Rufus, his boorish, foul-tempered son. The main problem with the first William's education was that he kept losing his teachers. Each time he appeared to be making a little academic headway someone would bump off his tutor. The first two were poisoned, the third was fatally wounded in a brawl and died of multiple stab wounds, and the fourth was savagely butchered in his bed only a few weeks after answering the advertisement. What the murderers did not realize in their haste to be off was that the twelve-year-old William was fast asleep in the same bed at the time and woke up to find himself drenched in his schoolmaster's blood. It was not an atmosphere conducive to higher education, particularly as at this time William was busily engaged in laying claim to his birthright, which was being fiercely disputed by the barons in the west of Normandy. William's father Robert, Duke of Normandy, had died inconveniently on a pilgrimage to Jerusalem leaving Herleve, the boy's mother (whom he had carelessly forgotten to marry before setting out), to do her best for the lad. Her best, as mentioned earlier, involved a great deal of fleeing and holing up in

118

shepherds' huts disguised as a peasant, for there was a price on the boy's head and few safe houses to afford a refuge.

There must have been some lulls in this stormy saga for we know that at the age of five William was provided with (as modern children might be given a box of toy soldiers) his own little company of boy soldiers to play with. At nine he and his infant regiment were acting out campaigns of Caesar's *Gallic Wars*, just as in later centuries his descendants imitated Marlborough, Wellington, and Field-Marshal Viscount Montgomery. Presumably one of William's literate lieutenants read out Caesar's words to him. The only real skill William learned from the mixture of pretend battles and real battles was survival.

If orthodox learning came hard to medieval princes, the more entertaining art of poetry was universally enjoyed. Itinerant minstrels and troubadours were always welcome in the banqueting halls. The little Richard II was taken by his uncle, John of Gaunt, to Warwick Castle for some ceremonial feast where the resident poet recited twelve thousand lines of blank verse which, if nothing else, shows how long our forebears took to eat their dinners. Henry I, nicknamed Beauclerc, was very fond of poetry and an amateur versifier himself. His grandson Henry II's education was also wide for the period. He learned the martial arts at Anjou, the contemporary equivalent of Sandhurst, which also taught its cadets courtly graces like serenading ladies and playing the lute. His scholastic education was supervised by the famous medieval grammarian Peter de Saintes and, when Henry came to England at the age of twelve to participate in his first grown-up battle, he snatched classes with a West Country monk from Bristol called Master Matthew.

Poetry was also the favourite schoolroom subject of the boy King, Henry III. He came to the throne aged nine and, by the time he was twelve, knew more about diplomatic wheeling and dealing than any modern politician with a lifetime's experience in Parliament. He wrote passable verse himself and it was during his reign that the post of Poet Laureate was introduced. The first person to get the job was a Master Henry to whom the King paid one hundred shillings to settle his debts before putting him on the permanent pay roll. His passion for poetry all but cost the King his life. A radical young poet called Ribald burst into the banqueting hall at Woodstock one evening, where the King was

119

dining with Queen Eleanor, and started declaring anti-monarchist and otherwise subversive rhyming couplets at the royal pair which, roughly paraphrased, said that Henry should abdicate and pass the crown over to Ribald, King of Poets. Instead of having the servants boot him out, Henry, tickled by the intruder's cheek, ordered them to take the versifier down to the kitchens and give him a good supper. Ribald regaled his below-stairs audience with more satirical verse, but when everyone had fallen asleep either from excess of alcohol or iambic pentameter, Ribald stole up to the King's chamber and hid under the rushes of the bed with dagger in his hand and regicide in his heart. His plan misfired. He fell asleep waiting for the King who, in any case, was that night sharing the Queen's bed. At midnight Ribald woke, leapt upon the bed, and murdered the bolster with suitable revolutionary curses which were heard by the virtuous Mistress Margaret Bisset, who was reading her Bible in a nearby chamber. She raised the alarm, Ribald was nabbed and clapped in irons. This time his poetry did not prevail. He was tried at the Coventry Assizes and afterwards suffered the unpoetic fate of being hanged, drawn, and quartered.

Henry III had a sensitive ear, not just for his own, but for all foreign languages. By the time he reached his teens it was said that he knew every language in Christendom and a few more besides. All boys, went the medieval adage, should learn manners and all boys should learn Latin. Latin was the language of diplomacy. Anyone hoping for a career in politics or in foreign affairs had to have Latin at his fingertips and a working knowledge of Italian, Spanish, and French. And a king who wished to deal personally with foreign emissaries needed all the current continental languages. But it was considered an extraordinary achievement when ten-year-old Princess Elizabeth Windsor held a brief and halting conversation with the French Ambassador in his own language at her father's coronation. Allowing for the fact that today many foreigners, particularly those meeting royalty, speak English, and that there is no incentive to learn other languages, with one or two exceptions the present Royal Family are poor linguists. Prince Michael of Kent is the only one who shows any natural flair for languages, with Russian, French, and German in his repertoire. His Austrian wife says she will bring her children up to be at least bilingual.

120

'If we are really to be members of the European Economic Community we should learn to speak at least some of the languages concerned,' says the Princess. 'In fact, we should all be more cosmopolitan in our attitudes.'

She added that at a party she had been to, given by Prince Charles, she was surprised not to find more foreigners. The Prince, she said, had a lot of predictably stuffy British friends. Medieval princesses were certainly cosmopolitan, marrying as they did into every European royal family.

A woodcut from Spiegel des menschlichen Lebens *by Rodericus Zamorensis, printed in 1475, and showing a schoolroom of the time of Edward IV*

Manners were considered as important in the medieval and Renaissance royal syllabus as book learning. A courtier without manners was a lute without strings, a pudding without plums. There were a rush of books about etiquette, the most comprehensive and the most influential in medieval times being *The Babees Boke* written in 1475 for the instruction of the 'six enfantes' at the court of Edward IV. Besides the Prince Edward, the Prince of Wales (later, as Edward V, one of the murdered Princes in the Tower), there were five other young children of noble birth to share the schoolroom at Ludlow Castle, including

121

Thomas Howard the future Duke of Norfolk. There were always extra children in royal households, for in those violent and unpredictable times orphans were common. It was not Christian charity alone that persuaded the monarch to offer shelter to the bereaved children of the nobility. Political strategy played its part. Useful marriages could be arranged between the offspring of warring families, to say nothing of estates to be acquired and houses appropriated. This was a time when children were betrothed in their cradles and married before they reached double figures. Even in the seventeenth century Mary Villiers, daughter of the Duke of Buckingham, was both wife and widow at the age of nine and climbed apple trees with her playmates, the Princesses Mary and Anne, in her widow's weeds.

The Babees Boke was directed specifically at children growing up in court which was the accepted centre of culture, courtesy, and chivalry and the rules laid down in it were designed to make little Lancelots of them all. The opening chapter deals with the proper behaviour at meals, not nursery tea as we know it, but the formal banquets in the Great Hall of Ludlow Castle or any other place where children of royal blood, or 'bele enfantes', would act as pages. It gives step by step, minute by minute advice. The child on entering the room should salute the lord, kneel on one knee, hold up his head, and say 'God speed'. He should listen attentively when addressed, but not chatter or stare about. He should stand until bidden to sit, answer respectfully, keep silent when the lord drank, and always maintain 'a blythe visage and a spirit diligent'.

These rules give us a rare picture of what those huge medieval meals were like. Pages had to keep a watchful eye on the high table to see if the lord required anything – water for his hands, a towel, a refill. If he offered the page a drink from his own cup the child was to take it with both hands and offer it to no one else. If the lord and lady were talking together the page should not interrupt and if he were praised for good behaviour he was to stand up and express his gratitude 'with demeanour meek but cheerful'.

It is not surprising that with all this busy, cheerful, diligent vigilance, the wretched page had no time to fill his own stomach, and *The Babees Boke* goes on to give further advice on conduct at his own meal. 'Burnish no bones with your teeth for that is unseemly,' it commands, 'nor stoop over your broth, dirty the cloth, drink when the mouth is full or pick nose or ears at table.' Scratching any part of the anatomy was forbidden. In short,

> Eat broth with a spoon, do not sup it, and do not leave the spoon in the dish, do not fill your mouth too full, and wipe it when you have drunk; do not dip your meat in the salt cellar nor put your knife in your mouth; taste of every dish but when your plate is taken away do not ask for it again; do not hack your meat like a labourer, have a clean knife and trencher for cheese, share with strangers of the best; when the meal is over clean your knives and put them away. Keep your seat till you have washed then go to the High Table and stand until Grace is said.

As meal-time manners they are as applicable now as five centuries ago. The book is all the more remarkable because it was written during one of the bloodiest periods of English history when the father of the chief 'babee' was fighting to keep his crown and his life. Let us for a moment forget Edward IV at his death, over-sexed and over-weight (though the actual cause of his death was the fatal chill he caught when out fishing), and remember instead the solicitous father who wanted his sons to grow up with books instead of battles. On his father's instructions the little Prince Edward's formal education began when he was three. His daily routine was rigorous, but affectionate. His father, fearing that his son's health was delicate, ordered an all night vigil to be kept over the boy's bed and a physician was permanently retained at the castle to mind him. Edward grew to be an accomplished pupil. By the time he was twelve William Caxton had dedicated several books to him and he was thought by contemporary observers to be exceptionally well-versed in all his subjects, particularly religion. It is sad to think that all this scholarship came to nothing more than a dismal death at the hands, in all probability, of his hunchback uncle Richard III.

A century earlier an equally solicitous father had tried to imbue the same love of scholarship in his son with less success. John of Gaunt, father of Henry IV, was a booklover and lifelong friend of the poet Geoffrey Chaucer who immortalized him in his poem 'The Boke of the Duchesse'. Gaunt is represented as the Man in Black. Young Henry had little time for schooling. Instead he followed his father from camp to camp on his various campaigns. Had his mother not died when he was three, things might have been different. Gaunt's first wife, his cousin Blanche, daughter of the Duke of Lancaster, was a beautiful and serious-minded woman revered by Chaucer as much as her husband and elegized in his work as the mysterious Whyte Lady.

In the Middle Ages and up to the end of the sixteenth century it was normal for children to be sent away from home at seven. They would serve in other households as pages, bower-maidens, or other domestic attendants, the less noble being allotted the more menial tasks. It was the medieval form of keeping up with the Joneses. A child from a farmer's house might be sent to the home of a wealthy landowner. The landowner's son would set his sights on a place in the service of a baron and so on up the social scale. Noble children were farmed out to the octopus branches of their families at home or abroad. Anne Boleyn and her sister Mary were brought up in the French court of Louis XII, whose wife Mary was the sister of Henry VIII. Anne had gone to France when she was eight, originally to the home of the Duchess of Savoy before moving on to higher things.

There was a darker fate for those children, usually the tail-enders of a large family, who could not find a suitably elevated foster home. For these the monasteries provided a permanent, but callous, refuge. Such children were called oblates and they could expect the harshest education of all. Oblation (also meaning sacrifice) was a handy way of disposing of surplus offspring at a time when the laws of primogeniture prevailed. John, youngest son of Henry II and Eleanor of Aquitaine, was offered as an oblate to an abbey in France at the age of seven. He was his mother's least favourite son: Eleanor blatantly favoured Richard (later Coeur de Lion) and would have left her last-born at the abbey forever had not Henry rescued him five years later. There is little doubt that John's ineptitude as a king was exacerbated by his formative years being spent in such unnatural conditions.

From a practical and theoretical point of view oblation was not a bad prospect for younger sons who did not have much to look forward to in the way of property or titles once their elder siblings had grabbed their share. Daughters too, the ugly and unmarriage-able ones at least, were thrown to the convents. The oblate system proved a useful form of recruitment for monasteries and convents because it allied the Church with some of the most powerful families in the land, as well as adding to the petty cash; oblates did not come empty-handed. The usual way was for the parent to present the child at five or six years to the chosen monastery. The handing over ceremony was awful and final. (John was one of the lucky ones who got out.) The parent would promise to relinquish the child permanently to holy orders and give some sort of bequest along with him – money or jewels or a portion of land. The child would then be stripped of his secular clothes, his cloak and his tunic, and would put on the garment that he would wear for the rest of his earthly life – the monk's cowl.

The pattern of his life would not alter a jot from that day onwards. He would be required to participate fully in the usual monastic discipline, its hourly devotions, the religious services, the work, the penances. He would be placed in the choir and have to learn the complicated chants that accompanied the services. It was the common boast, made presumably by the monks themselves, that no king's son was more carefully reared than the least of boys in a well-ordered monastery, not a difficult boast to fulfil since several sons of monarchs *were* the least of boys in these religious communities.

Monastic life in medieval times was harsh. Victorian boarding schools described by Dickens are holiday camps by comparison. Every oblate was assigned a pupil-master or guardian and these sinister, cowled men were instructed always to be with them like shadows, to sit, stand, and sleep between them, never allowing the children to have physical contact. Any form of human recognition, a smile, a nod, a handclasp, was denied the oblate. They could not hand over a hymn book or a plate of food for fear that their hands should touch and carnal pleasure be derived. Everything was done through a middleman, the abbot, the prior, or one of the guardians. No monk other than the oblate's master was permitted near him – no bad rule this, bearing in mind the lascivious nature of some of the older inmates. The oblates slept in dormitories bleaker even than those up at Gordonstoun in Prince Philip's day. Between the beds were the beds of the ubiquitous masters, and one of these would keep vigil all night by candlelight to ensure that the children got up to no mischief. They were escorted to and from the latrines and regularly beaten, though not for any particular crime. (God knows, with all this supervision there could scarcely have been an opportunity to bite a thumbnail or scratch a toe without detection.) Flogging was part of the regular curriculum. One vexed Abbot complained to Anselm, Archbishop of Canterbury at the turn of the eleventh century and later canonized, about the wilful and high-spirited nature of the little boys in his care.

'We never give over beating them day and night', he declared, 'and they only get worse and worse.'

Anselm, one of the leading reformists of his day and passionately against raising this form of infant conscript army into the clergy, replied:

'Are they not human? Are they not flesh and blood like you? Would you like to have been treated as you treat them and to have become what they are now?'

Flogging for all children, royals as well, was commonplace. The boy King Henry vi who presided over his first Privy Council at the age of nine months sitting on his mother's knees, his crown atop his bald baby head, was regularly beaten by his guardian, Richard Beauchamp, Earl of Warwick. Fearing repercussions from the adult King in later life, Warwick asked the council 'truly to assist him in the exercise of the charge and occupation that he hath about the king's person, namely in chastising of him for his defaults'. A classic case of 'united we stand'. A whipping-boy, the contemporary of a prince introduced into the royal nursery to bear the brunt of his punishment, was clearly not used in Henry's case. The physical disciplining of children was savage and hardly changed from the Middle Ages to the middle of this present century. It is the field in which least progress was made. Girls were no exceptions. Lady Jane Grey claimed that her parents, Lord and Lady Dorset, later the Duke and Duchess of Suffolk, gave her 'nips and bobs' and beat her 'most cruelly' when she failed to do their bidding. The most famous whipping-boy was Barnaby Fitzpatrick, an engaging red-headed Irish lad who was one of Edward vi's playmates, but there is no real evidence to support the theory that Master Fitzpatrick was the surrogate victim. Roger Ascham, one of the Tudor tutors famous for his liberal leanings, was nevertheless a great believer in a little judicious beating to encourage a recalcitrant child to learn.

Beating instruments over the centuries have included whips, canes, birches, iron rods, leather belts, cats-of-nine-tails, and the

126

'discipline' which was a small bundle of chains; a particularly sadistic device was the flapper, of which Victorian schoolmasters were fond. It was a leather strap with a pear-shaped thong at one end, into which a small hole had been cut. If applied with sufficient force it could raise large blisters on the victim's bare skin. One meticulous nineteenth-century schoolmaster estimated that he had in his distinguished academic career administered to several generations of pupils 911,527 strokes with the stick, 124 lashes with the whip, 136,715 slaps with the hand, and 1,111,800 boxes on the ear. Beethoven, notoriously short-tempered when teaching slow students, would whip them with a knitting needle and occasionally bit them. A favourite method of chastisement popular in monasteries (yet another thorn in the wretched oblate's flesh) was to prick the soles of a child's feet with an instrument of the sort cobblers use for stitching tough hide.

Imagine for a moment the lack of privacy in medieval castles, where everyone shared a communal room – parents, servants, guests, and children – and it is not difficult to see why this savage kind of therapy started so young. The battered-baby syndrome is as old as time, its practice encouraged by the highest and mightiest. The seventeenth-century infant Louis XIII, who grew up to be a depraved sexual deviant, was used to regular whipping by his father from the age of two. At seventeen months he could be quelled from a childish tantrum by the mere sight of the heavy leather thong that hung by his father's side. From two onwards he would be given regular floggings every morning. On the morning of his coronation, no exception was allowed and the wretched child was heard to whimper, 'I would rather do without so much obeisance and honour if they would not have me whipped'. The terrible nightmares that the child King suffered as a result of this continuous physical abuse lasted well into his adult life and probably accounted for most of his perversions. Public schools have long had a vicious reputation for flogging which only the last twenty years have seen decline. The most notorious headmaster of Eton was the Elizabethan academic, Nicholas Udall, who was fond of using four apple-twigs bound together into a lash. So many boys ran away from Eton in his day because of the flogging that the matter was taken up by the Secretary of State, William Cecil.

Let us leave the brutal face of education and consider an altogether cheerier subject – music. We have been blessed with many

127

'The Music Party' by Philippe Mercier, showing Frederick, Prince of Wales, and his three eldest sisters in a state of rare harmony. The Prince is playing the violoncello, Anne, Princess Royal is seated at the harpsichord, Caroline plucks the mandora and Amelia is reading a copy of Milton musically gifted princes and princesses. Princess Mary, George v's daughter, had such a fine soprano voice that Dame Nellie Melba, who heard her sing in an impromptu concert, said that the Princess, given different circumstances, could have made opera her career. How much flannel and flattery this judgement contained is anyone's guess, but the Princess was accomplished enough to give small private concerts at the Palace, to which Dame Nellie brought her operatic friends. It was an altogether different story with Princess Charlotte, eldest daughter of George III. She detested music and played truant from her harpsichord lessons at Chiswick, where she and her twelve siblings were brought up. It was not entirely cussedness: she was thought to be tone deaf. She wrote a rebellious letter to her brother Augustus Frederick the night before her first ball, declaring that she would probably fall asleep with boredom before the evening was out, for her dislike of dancing was almost as intense. The ball was even worse than she had feared. Charlotte was in such agony of shyness when invited to dance in public for the first time that she tripped and lost her shoe. It prompted the following ditty which began:

> *Alas where is my shoe.*
> *The Princess hopped,*
> *The musicians stopped*
> *Not knowing what to do . . .*

which later became the children's nursery rhyme

> *Cocka doodle doo,*
> *My dame has lost her shoe.*
> *My master's lost his fiddling stick*
> *And doesn't know what to do.*

A few hundred years earlier, however, the young Henry VIII had shown such a talent for music and dancing that his parents allowed him to stay up late to take part in evening entertainments. At seven he was given his own troop of musicians and directed childish revels at Eltham Palace. He played the lute, virginals, and dulcimer, had a pleasing singing voice, and was a competent composer, but his favourite activity was dancing. He was a tireless performer, inviting the ladies-in-waiting to dance in as courtly a manner as any older gallant. The Tudors, with their Welsh blood, were all natural musicians. Henry's sister Mary, who later married the French King, was at the age of eight an expert on the virginals and also a small organ called a royal. One afternoon the Venetian Ambassador and envoys arrived at the palace for an audience with the King and Queen who, for some reason, were not available. The eight-year-old Princess invited the Signor and his party to the music room, where she entertained them on the virginals for an hour to their great surprise and delight. The audience applauded and rose to take their leave. Princess Mary politely requested them to return to their seats and, by way of an encore, demonstrated her prowess on the lute for another hour. The Ambassador and his retinue were finally released and the dazed Italian complimented the Queen on her talented little daughter, promising to send her the finest lute in all of Venice.

Elizabeth Tudor was also a skilful lute player and keyboard musician, and inherited her father's talent for dancing. She was a beautiful dancer both to partner and to watch and, at sixty, still cut a graceful figure on the dance floor. But it is Elizabeth's academic achievement that makes her such a special royal child and, without doubt, the best-educated of our sovereigns. Fashions in education, as in everything else, change over the years with some tutors favouring classics, others languages, others history or religious studies, and others dwelling principally on the social graces. The difference in emphasis is obvious when we compare the timetables of the two Queen Elizabeths. In 1936 Marion Crawford, the royal governess at Buckingham Palace, drew up the following timetable for the ten-year-old Princess Elizabeth of York, who had just become Heir Presumptive. It went thus:

	Monday	Tuesday	Wednesday	Thursday	Friday
09.30	Bible-reading	Arithmetic	Arithmetic	Arithmetic	Arithmetic
10.00	History	Grammar	Geography	History	Writing composition
11.00	Milk and biscuits				
11.30 to lunch	half: silent reading while Crawfie corrected her written work; half: reading aloud from such classics as Dickens, Thackeray and Jane Austen. Her favourite was *Persuasion*.				

130

Princesses Elizabeth and Margaret Rose at their lessons at Windsor, June 1940

After lunch the Princess and her younger sister would occupy the afternoons with singing, music, drawing, and dancing – Madame Vacani came to the Palace to give ballet lessons. Friday afternoon activities were particularly light with the family preparing to drive to Royal Lodge, Windsor for the weekend.

Queen Mary was shown the timetable and didn't think much of it. Far too much arithmetic, she said, and not enough Bible-reading or learning poetry by heart. She also recommended more history and genealogical studies; so important to find out all about one's royal ancestors, declared Grandmother. As usual Granny got her way; several of the arithmetic lessons were scratched in favour of poetry reading and, when she was thirteen, the Princess spent one afternoon a week at Windsor learning Constitutional History from Sir Henry Marten, Vice-Provost of Eton. The little

> *Think your*
> *Country your home', the'inhabitants*
> *your neighbours, all freinds your*
> *children, and your children your*
> *own Sowl; endeuouring to surpass*
> *all these' in liberality and good*
> *nature'.*

Elizabeth Tudor's handwritten translation of a dialogue between Hiero and Simonides in Xenophon

girl would sit in a corner of his cheerful, chintzy drawing-room full of books and bric-à-brac, gazing up at the ceiling while Sir Henry spelled out the finer points of parliamentary law and why there needed to be someone called Black Rod to introduce Members of the Commons to the House of Lords. Miss Crawford sat in the hall outside reading her favourite author, P.G. Wodehouse. Both her mother and grandmother were anxious that Elizabeth should be accomplished in artistic rather than academic subjects. Queen Mary would take her granddaughter on afternoon excursions to galleries such as the Wallace Collection, just north of Oxford Street, where they would pace about the rooms for hours. As for her mother, Queen Elizabeth, she simply did not see the need for the girl to be proficient in higher mathematics and told Miss Crawford so. Her mother's academic insouciance rubbed off on her elder daughter who was once asked what she would like to be when she grew up. A lady living in the country with lots of horses and dogs, she said.

The schoolroom at Buckingham Palace was kindergarten compared to the timetable allotted to the first Queen Elizabeth by her tutor Roger Ascham. Classics and modern languages were the bread and butter of the Tudor Princess's scholastic diet. She read Greek in the mornings – Socrates, Demosthenes, Sophocles, and the Greek Testament. She read Latin in the afternoons – 'most of Cicero, all of Livy, and especially the poetry of Horace and Catullus. In fact, she read classics for sheer pleasure. When she became Queen and her school days were officially finished, Ascham was retained as her Latin secretary. After supper for relaxation they would read Greek together. She learned to speak fluent French, Spanish, and Italian and passable German and always spoke directly to foreign envoys without an interpreter, a great asset for a well-informed monarch. Ascham was justifiably proud of his pupil and wrote in his famous book *The Schoolmaster*, addressing the young gentlemen of England: 'It is your shame that one maid should go beyond you all in excellence of learning and knowledge of divers tongies.'

When she became Queen, Elizabeth appointed Sir Nicholas Bacon as senior court tutor and asked him to draw up a timetable for the education of the wards of court. He came up with the following programme, which did not even allow the children time for breakfast. Immediately after morning chapel, they were to settle down with their Latin grammars and not lift their heads until eleven when dinner was served. During the two hours after the meal the Greek master would teach them, after which came an hour of French to chivvy their spirits, before once again they were plunged into the classics until five o'clock. This was the hour for evening prayers whereupon the children, who must by now have had their eyelids propped open, were allowed to indulge in their own interests until it was eight o'clock and time for bed.

There was still a preoccupation with the overall demeanour of a growing child – the way he bore himself, stood at table, ate his food, doffed his cap. Even Erasmus, who was so impressed with the work of Lady Jane Grey and corresponded with the young bluestocking in Latin, brought out one of these Books of Urbanity as they were known, full of useful advice for children who wished to appear well mannered.

Let not thy nosethrills [nostrils] be full of snivel like a sluttish person . . . to dry it on the cape of the coat or on thine elbow is the propriety of the fishmonger. It is good manners to dry it

with thy handkerchief and that with thy head turned somewhat aside if more honest persons be present.

In royal history there was no better schooling both for excellence of teaching and brilliance of pupil than that of the Tudor schoolroom in the decade of the 1540s. Prince Edward, Princess Elizabeth, and Lady Jane Grey were all prodigies by our standards. Compared with their contemporaries, their achievements are less extraordinary, for this was the Renaissance when learning was considered to be a joy as well as a necessity. The prejudices against educating women, which had prevailed in the Middle Ages, where, unless a girl was destined for the convent, she would not be taught Latin, were everywhere being toppled. It was no longer felt, as had been said, that to give women education was to give a madman a sword.

An Italian male chauvinist wrote that if you taught women Latin you would simply open the door for them to be able to read the amorous nonsense of Boccaccio, or worse, the erotic verses of

The Family of Henry VIII: the King sits enthroned with his son, the future Edward VI, and his third Queen, Jane Seymour: Princess Mary stands on the left, and Princess Elizabeth on the right

Ovid. Were they to study music the moral fibre of their character would be undermined, or worse, they would be seduced by their music masters. All their teachers must, of course, be female. Fortunately, these prophecies fell on stony ground. Renaissance women were outstanding scholars. Thomas More's three daughters and their cousin Margaret Griggs, who lived with the family, were insatiable readers of the classics. Having visited them at home in Chelsea, Erasmus said afterwards that it was like visiting the Academy of Plato. Across the Channel in Europe the same situation pertained. In Spain during this period there were two female university professors, a professor of Latin in Salamanca and a professor of history at Alcala, a phenomenon which was not to be repeated until the twentieth century. Catherine of Aragon was so determined that her daughter Mary should be well-educated that she sent home for the famous Spanish classicist Juan Luis Vives to be the little Princess's tutor. Vives proceeded to write an austere treatise on the subject of education called *The Instruction of Christian Women* which would have made suitable bedside reading for a Trappist monk. Well-educated young women, said the author, should not indulge in any of the things that warm the vulgar, female heart, worldly pleasures should be avoided, no pretty clothes, no jewellery, no scent, no make-up. Proper young ladies refused fancy foods and wine, they did not dance or play loose parlour games. They should not sleep too long, talk too much or laugh loudly and when out walking should be veiled and avoid the company and especially the eyes of young men. A respectable young woman's time was best employed at home with a female chaperone reading edifying literature. Relenting slightly, Vives conceded that instead of drinking plain water a young woman might be permitted to drink ale.

Vives followed up this bestseller with another. It was written in Latin and called *Satellitium* (The Bodyguard) and was, in short, a Pocket Guide to Priggishness. It consisted of 239 pithy mottoes, many not more than five words long, designed to keep the nine-year-old Princess on the straight and narrow. A random selection will give an idea of its head-prefect's tone. 'No complaints', 'War upon vice', 'The more fortune smiles, the less she should be trusted', 'Nobility lies not in birth but in virtue', etc. When she became Queen and burned bishops for breakfast, Bloody Mary suffered (hardly surprisingly) from insomnia and would read herself to sleep with her little manual on maidenly morality.

The Tudors had some weird and some wonderful teachers who must, surely, in Lord Melbourne's words have moulded and directed their characters. Henry VIII's tutor John Skelton was almost as colourful a character as his pupil was destined to become. He was a Cambridge scholar, famous for his satirical verses. He composed a short ditty about his time in the royal schoolroom which starts:

> *The Honour of England I learned to spell,*
> *I gave him drink of the sugared well*
> *Of Hellicon's waters crystalline,*
> *Acquainting him with the Muses nine . . .*

Henry could turn a neat verse himself when he became older, but that was the only courtly grace his Bohemian and wild-mannered governor taught him. Fortunately there were enough Books of

Urbanity kicking about, such as *The Babees Boke* and *Stans Puer ad Mensam* (The Boy Standing at the Table), leaving Skelton free to concentrate his energies on the more formal aspects of education. When he left royal service he became a Norfolk clergyman and scandalized his parishioners, in the pulpit by his ungodly ranting against Cardinal Wolsey, and at home where he had taken a common-law wife.

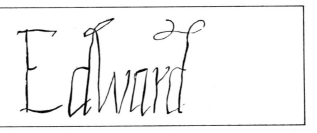

Edward VI's signature

Edward vi's first teacher, Richard Cox, was a more orthodox Mister-Chips figure who drummed Latin syntax into his young pupil by pretending the text was a battle; maybe one of his father's recent campaigns like Boulogne would be enacted with the different parts of speech becoming the French enemy. It worked well. In a report sent by Cox to Archbishop Cranmer on the child's progress (a remarkable document, because it shows how much a nine-year-old was able to assimilate), Edward's tutor wrote:

> He hath learned almost four books of Cato to construe, to parse and say without book. And of his own coining now in the latter book he will needs have at one time fourteen verses which he conneth pleasantly and perfectly besides things of the Bible, the *Satilitium*, of Aesop's *Fables*, and Latin making.

Cox was extremely impressed with Edward's intellect, describing him to his father as 'a vessel apt to receive all goodness and learning, witty, sharp and pleasant'.

The teacher that followed Cox was very different. John Cheke was a radical. Brilliant, fiery, outspoken, Cheke became Regius

Professor of Greek at Cambridge at the extraordinarily youthful age of twenty-six and was the moving spirit of a pro-Protestant faction there, whose disciples included both Elizabeth's future tutors, Roger Ascham and William Grindal, as well as the two men who were appointed to tutor Lady Jane Grey, John Aylmer and John Haddon. Cheke was the undisputed leader of the academic radical clique and was considered by many a little too turbulent for the job of dealing with Edward when Henry selected him. Cheke was not the indulgent, battle-game simulator that Cox had been and set about the business of educating Edward in the classics in the manner of a professor giving tutorials nowadays, talking to the seven-year-old as one adult to another, getting him to write compositions in Latin and Greek pertaining to topical subjects, never talking down to him or flattering him. By the time he was twelve Edward had read all Cicero and Livy, pretty good going considering how much else in the way of academic meat was being heaped on his plate. He was fluent in French by the age of fourteen (he wrote a cheery little thesis in it on one vital contemporary issue entitled 'Treatise against the Supremacy of the Pope') and in Italian and Spanish as well as Latin and Greek. He was enthusiastic about geography and could, it was said, tell an audience of bemused and impressed adults exactly what ships with what cargoes were lying at which ports of his kingdom. This, at least, shows some glimmer of normality in this stuffed piglet, for he grew to be immensely interested in expeditions and explorations, so beloved in later years by his half-sister Elizabeth. He sponsored an expedition to the Arctic under the leadership of Hugh Willoughby which left England only a few weeks before Edward died.

The Renaissance enthusiasm did not stop at London. Up in the gloomy halls of Stirling Castle little James VI got more than his fair share of the academic cake. When he was four, eight full-time teachers were appointed to supervise his schooling, two tutors, two music masters, two physical education instructors (to teach him military prowess, riding, hunting, shooting, and falconry), and two language teachers (French and Italian). There was also a part-time dancing master. His chief tutor was the internationally renowned Scottish classicist, George Buchanan, who spoke fluent Latin (with a Highland accent) and whose Latin prose had been favourably compared to Livy and Virgil.

James was stuffed with facts like a turkey with sage and onion. Buchanan's opinion, and he was a man of violent opinions upheld to the death, was that a monarch should be the wisest man in the realm and wisdom meant facts. First priority was given to the library which was stocked with enough books to satisfy a university. His timetable was as grim and forbidding as the castle in which the little chap grew up. It began with prayers at 5.30 a.m., followed by three hours of Greek, then breakfast at nine, followed by three hours of Latin. After lunch James studied languages, cosmography (which included geography and astronomy), and afterwards, by way of light relief, a couple of hours' worth of dialectics and rhetoric. He wasn't much good at oratory because his tongue was too big for his mouth which gave him a lisp and an unattractive tendency to spit when he spoke. Somewhere in all this his fencing, riding, and battle practice had to be fitted, to say nothing of a twirl about the dance floor, learning complicated quadrilles, and a session on the lute with one of the two music masters. There was also the small matter of ruling Scotland. Because he had succeeded to the throne as a baby after his mother's forced abdication, he was required to fulfil the odd monarchical duty such as presiding over the Privy Council or opening Parliament. When this happened he would be snatched from his Greek or his dialectics, kitted out in purple robes and ermine train, and escorted to the Great Chamber by a bevy of lairds. When James was eight the curious Queen Elizabeth despatched an envoy, Sir Henry Killigrew, up to Scotland to investigate her royal neighbour. Killigrew reported back by letter that the child was a living lexicon. He spoke French so well that Killigrew, whose own French was poor, had sent for the French Ambassador to put him through his paces. James had not merely passed muster but passed with flying colours, amazing both men with his polished prose. The oral examination over, James sat a written paper. Killigrew picked a chapter from the Bible himself (to make sure there was no cheating), and the child was asked to translate it from Latin to French, from French into English and from English back into Latin. Full marks again. The final test was dancing. A small orchestra was summoned, the carpets rolled back, and the dazed and dazzled Killigrew was forced to admit that the boy executed the steps with much grace.

The result of all this hot-house attention was predictable and

Prince Charles arriving at Kings Cross Station on his way home for Christmas from Gordonstoun in 1962

inevitable. James became an insufferable little prig. He loved to cap a remark with a quotation from the Bible (which he knew by heart) or a long-winded pun. Peter Young, one of his tutors, collected up the little beast's pithier quotations and put them into a book which for dullness rivals a railway timetable. Small wonder he came to be called 'the British Solomon' and 'the wisest fool in Christendom'.

The wheel has turned full circle. British kings have returned to Scotland for their education. Both the present Prince of Wales and his father were educated at Gordonstoun, near Inverness. Prince

Charles will be the first British monarch to have been to public school. When the Queen made her decision to send him away to boarding school it was assumed he would go to Eton, traditionally the training ground for children of the nobility. Why, apart from the fact that her husband was an old boy, the Queen chose Gordonstoun is a mystery. It is way down the list for academic achievement and has no record at all as a sporting school. Other Scottish public schools send their second or third fifteens to play rugger at Gordonstoun. The one word that sums up (or rather *summed* up for times have changed and fitted carpets and central heating have now encroached, even into Inverness) the character of the school is 'rugged'. When Prince Charles was there he joined the school coastguard service. Whenever the short sharp blasts of the warning siren rang out, indicating that a boat was in distress, he and his fellow coastguards would drop everything, even jump out of bed if it went off at night, scramble into their navy blue duffle coats, and race up to the coastguard station on the cliff top to keep watch. Had he wanted, Charles could have joined the school fire brigade or ambulance corps, but the coastguards were the most fun. There was cliff-rescue practice and life-boat drill and more opportunity for smuggling a bottle of some warming liquor, cherry brandy or twelve-year-old malt, into one's pocket to keep the chill out of young bones without being observed. Both Charles's brothers have been junior coastguards, though these days long trousers, instead of the famous Gordonstoun all-weather shorts, make cliff-top watches in February more palatable. Gordonstoun boys still run a couple of miles before breakfast, but cold showers are a thing of the past. The most famous and innovative aspect of the schooling is its punishment system. There is no official punishment. Instead of black marks, minutes are meted out to the culprit – two minutes for talking after lights out, three minutes for being late for assembly, ten minutes for smoking behind the bicycle shed. At the end of the week the minutes are totted up and the wretched boy must then forgo whatever Saturday entertainment he had planned, a football match, tea with parents, an outing, and spend a couple of hours, or however many minutes' worth of crimes he has accumulated, on a cross-country walk. The punishments are not supervised. The boys are put on their honour and trusted to complete them. And do they?

'Of course,' said an old boy now in the champagne trade, virtuously.

'Certainly not,' said an old boy now working as a rock-and-roll drummer, 'not if you had any sense. The clever boys all skived.'

Skiving was an art in which Prince Henry, James I's elder son, was an expert. Here begins the great decline in royal education which did not return to any pinnacle until Prince Albert set down the rules for his family's schooling. But the decline was gradual. Prince Henry may have been the opposite of his fact-finding, book-loving father, even though he was an enthusiastic art-collector. He liked playing soldiers better than anything else. As a child he would spend six or seven hours dressed in armour going for long walks to prepare himself for forced marches. Gordonstoun punishments would have suited him well. Even his musical tastes were martial. There was nothing he liked better than trumpets and drums, and the sound or a cannon roaring was music to his ears. This rankled with his father, who loathed anything smacking of brute force and shuddered at the sight of a uniform. Henry was also fascinated by naval practices and spent many happy afternoons nosing round the dockyards quizzing the royal shipwrights. His other great passion was tennis. Hunting, so favoured by his father (James would cancel council meetings to hunt), he despised. He played tennis three or four hours a day and shocked his governor by stripping down to his shirt when on court. It was this favourite sport that brought about his premature death, for when playing tennis at eighteen he caught a chill which proved fatal (though we should mention the rumours that he was poisoned, conceivably even by his own father).

Waiting on the substitute's bench when Henry died was baby Charles, another indifferent student. His father had been so shaken by his elder son's unexpected death (or so disgusted at his behaviour in life) that he seemed to care little how his second son was educated. Alas, had Charles been taught to use his head more, he might have kept it. The carefree feeling rubbed off on Charles who, in turn, demanded a far less academic training for his own children. Charles II's tutor, William Cavendish Earl of Newcastle, was briefed by the King to concentrate less on academic than on social and political matters. Ironically, considering Charles I's demise, the ability to get on with and handle people was now the aim. Cavendish set no great store by

142

books. The junior Charles, he declared, should study things not words, matter not language. In fact, too much study of any kind was a bad thing since contemplation got in the way of action. 'The greatest clerks', said Cavendish 'are not the greatest men.' Charles was certainly no great clerk. From an early age he preferred ladies to Latin and was once slapped on the head by his father for ogling and giggling with the lading during a sermon in church. One exasperated, but obviously affectionate tutor, wrote of his pupil: 'He kisses and loves all and when the smart of the rod is past, smiles on his beater.' As for his younger brother James, he made no pretence to any academic interest whatsoever and was left to pick up what he could, which was hardly more than a smattering of the classics. He was very good at loading guns.

The Renaissance ideal had died and was not to be revived for another two hundred years. James's daughters, Mary and Anne, both future queens (though no one ever supposed they would succeed), were brought up to be assets to the drawing-room. They had a French master who taught them polite conversation and enough grammar to enable them to read French novels. But their favourite French master was their dancing master, who taught them the latest dances from Paris. Sumuel Pepys writes glowingly in his diary of Princess Mary's facility in the ballroom. He watched her 'dance most finely so as almost to ravish one – her ears were so good'. Their official tutor was the Bishop of London, who spoke more like a colonel than a bishop. The accepted hierarchical pattern for royal educators became an aristocratic governor, an ecclesiastic tutor, and several university professors from Oxford and Cambridge as the actual teachers. Below these were drawing, dancing, music, and riding teachers. Mary and Anne were typical schoolgirls, loving make-up and pretty clothes and having crushes upon older girls. For Mary it was Frances Apsley, daughter of the King's Receiver-General and nine years older than the Princess. For Anne, a more impressionable child, the crush proved to be more disastrous and permanent. The object of her passion was Sarah Jennings, the future Duchess of Malborough, who completely dominated the timid Princess. Sarah boasted that she had never read a book in her life, played cards all the time, even on Sunday, and if Anne had any sense she would follow her example.

Substitute riding horses for playing cards and that advice could well apply to the recently elected Chancellor of London University, the present Princess Anne. She told a friend and fellow pupil of Guildford House at Benenden, after they had finished their 'O' levels, that she felt like packing up all her school-books into a carrier bag and chucking them into the Thames. An even less distinguished scholar than Princess Anne was the present Princess of Wales. At the age of twelve she was sent to West Heath near Sevenoaks, a smart girls' boarding school noted for social rather than intellectual achievement. Unlike her sister-in-law at Benenden, Diana was never bossy or noisy or bumptious, but rather diffident and retiring. Her popularity was due perhaps to her good looks and prowess at games, certainly not to her academic record. Contemporaries remember her blushing furiously when reprimanded for having more than thirty mistakes in a short French translation, or for having studiously written a history essay on 'Edward the Lionheart'. She left West Heath with no 'O' levels for a finishing school in Switzerland, still remembering the watchword of the headmistress of her preparatory school, Riddlesworth Hall in Diss, not far from her childhood home in Sandringham, 'We like our girls to learn to face forward'.

After the impeccable standards set by the Tudors, the education allotted to their successors was largely cosmetic until the time thirty years ago when Princess Alexandra was sent to Heathfield, becoming the first royal princess to go to boarding school. The six little princesses Charlotte, Elizabeth, Augusta, Mary, Sophia, and Amelia, who made up the distaff side of George III's surviving brood of thirteen, had the typical education afforded to blue-blooded females of that period. Under the overall supervision of Lady Charlotte Finch, or 'Cha' as she was affectionately called, a stream of teachers passed through the schoolroom attempting to drum a little knowledge into their pupils. There was Miss Goldsworthy (the King called her 'Gooly') who taught them mathematics, Madame Montmollins, nicknamed 'La Mont', who had formerly been employed by the Russian royal family, who taught them French. There was a sub-governess called Mary Hamilton from Scotland who was seduced by the Prince of Wales in between teaching them needlework, an elderly and flirtatious clergyman called Charles de la Guiffardière who taught them dancing, and a governess called Miss Gomm who taught them how to embroider and to do purse-netting, bead-work, and tapestry. (Royal parents have always favoured tapestry for their children from William I's Queen, Matilda, to the Duke of Windsor and George VI, both experts at *gros point*, taught to them by their mother Queen Mary.) They had a social teacher, M. Desmoyer, to show them how to manage their hooped skirts and trains, and no less than four art instructors. Miss Black taught them crayon work, Mr Cooper specialized in landscape painting, a Signor Rebecca taught them figure drawing, and a Flemish gentleman by the name of Rustan gave them special coaching on the correct way to draw heads, hands, and feet in chalk.

Their education was not serious, which was just as well for, apart from Princess Sophia, they were not overloaded with brains. At least, said an observer, this preoccupation with embroidery needles and paint brushes is better than a preoccupation for gaming, novels, and intrigues. Only Sophia showed any real aptitude for languages. In her old age she lost her sight and employed four readers who would each read to her for an hour in English, French, German, and Italian. Princess Charlotte (the tone-deaf daughter who lost her shoe) had the best handwriting and wrote the best English composition. Augusta shone at music and playing cricket with her seven brothers. Mary relied on her looks and her faultless manners. Elizabeth was called the Muse by her family because of her talent for art, and poor Amelia, the after-thought, twenty-one years younger than the Prince of Wales, just about managed to read and write. They were all excellent needlewomen and the various royal establishments overflowed with hand-stitched cushions, samplers, chair covers, and tablecloths. Sadly, none of them had any children (legitimate at least; Princess Sophia had a bastard son whose father was never conclusively identified) for whom they might have embroidered pretty layettes.

At least if they weren't brilliant, Queen Charlotte's six daughters were more or less biddable. Princess Charlotte, the daughter of the Prince Regent, was, to put it mildly, a difficult child. Governesses came and went. Charlotte screamed, stamped her foot, tore her books, refused to be taught German by the gentle Mr Kuper on the grounds that he was a spy, and wrote to a friend that one of her sub-governesses, a Mrs Udney, was 'really beyond everything I ever knew. Contempt is not sufficient for her for I

145

Caroline, Princess of Wales, with her daughter, Princess Charlotte. Thomas Lawrence's painting is highly idealistic: Princess Caroline was far from the serene, beautiful harpist he has portrayed, while Princess Charlotte proved a difficult, spoilt child, although she did take to music with enthusiasm

now dislike and I am disgusted with her.' Mrs Udney used to spank Charlotte, which was no bad thing in the circumstances. The only subject that the Princess took to without coercion was music. She learned to play the guitar which had just come into fashion. She was particularly attracted to the flamenco and with a violinist and a cellist borrowed from the King's orchestra she staged small entertainments for her friends. It was not sheer bad temper that made her difficult; her eccentric domestic arrangements must have had a damaging effect on her character too. George and Caroline, her father and mother, were not on speaking terms and had separated even before she was born. The governesses appointed by her mother were sacked by her father, and vice-versa. Some of the teachers were as difficult as the pupil they had come to teach. One, Miss Cornelia Knight, objected to the title of governess, preferring the more genteel description lady companion, and wrote letters to the newspapers demanding that they use her correct professional title. Eventually a male tutor was despatched to take Charlotte in hand, a Dr George Nott, who was appalled at her laziness, her slovenly spelling, illegible handwriting, and general academic incompetence. Charlotte was, after all, destined to be queen, there being no other legitimate heir among George III's thirteen children. After the exasperated Dr Nott had set her an essay in which she had fifty spelling mistakes, he was prompted to write her a cautionary note which went as follows:

> Where, may I ask your Royal Highness, is this to end, or when are we to have the satisfaction of seeing your mind animated with a becoming pride and a generous resolution to improve? More than three months have passed during which the most unremitting exertions have been employed by those about you, and what is the progress you have made? Let the enclosed paper speak. I shall only add that ignorance is disgraceful in proportion to the rank of the person in whom it is found and that negligence, when the means of improvement are in your power, is criminal in the sight of the Almighty.

Charlotte was deeply distressed at this rebuke and swore passionately that she would do better.

While he lasted, Dr Nott made sizeable inroads into her education, but political intrigue between her parents' warring factions prevailed and he was removed. An anonymous book entitled *Hints towards Forming the Character of a Young Princess* was published soon afterwards, not by Dr Nott, but by Ms Hannah More, a highly intelligent contemporary feminist and one-time crony of Dr Johnson who many hoped would take over Charlotte's education. Sadly this was not to be. The Princess was appointed more male clerics, none of whom dealt with her high spirits and fiery temper with much success.

Temper was not something that Princess Victoria's tutor had to contend with, for as a child Victoria was sweet-tempered, if strong-willed. She did her lessons entirely alone under the supervision first of Baroness Lehzen (who had been with the Kent

A sketch of Victoria and Albert with their three eldest children. The Prince is portrayed teaching the alphabet to Albert Edward, Prince of Wales. Prince Albert's plans for the education of his eldest son were not to proceed as smoothly as this early lesson

family for years as a sort of nanny-cum-companion) and later under Dr Davys, Dean of Chester. She was a diligent, if un-exciting, scholar except in one respect; she excelled in drawing, as her later paintings demonstrate. Her Albert himself created the programme of study for their eldest son, Albert Edward, the Prince of Wales. It consisted of a six-hour day covering nine different subjects with an hour each for languages and half an hour for the others. The curriculum included religion, English, writing, French, music, calculating, German, drawing, and geography. The trouble with Albert Edward's education lay not so much in what his tutors, Henry Mildred Birch and Frederick Weymouth Gibbs, taught him, but in the over-ambitious goal that Prince Albert and his henchman Baron Stockmar had set for him. They wanted the Prince of Wales to be the Perfect Man and the ordinary mortal fell short of the mark. So scarred was Edward VII by his idealistic, inhuman upbringing that his own sons Albert

Victor (Eddy) and George was given a softer ride. Neither of them was very clever and both were shunted into naval careers which have become the trademark of royal education for boys today – all the Queen's sons having been either in or heading for the senior service.

The awkward, knock-kneed schoolboy Albert, who by accident was to become George vi, became a less willing sailor. His parents had great fears that he wouldn't pass the entrance exam to the Royal Naval College at Dartmouth, where his father and grandfather had both been cadets, and where his elder brother Edward had also done well. George, Bertie to his family, spent most of his childhood in the shadow of his charismatic elder brother and, from the first, was treated as an also-ran. The children's first nanny at York Cottage, the family's unpretentious home on the Sandringham estate, was so biased towards Edward that she seriously undernourished little Bertie, and even in his teens, he had problems with his digestion. Bertie became a shy, nervous boy with a stutter that grew to be a definite speech impediment and his father's constant nagging did not help matters. His serious education began when he was six. He and Edward had just spent eight months living with their grandfather (now Edward vii) at Buckingham Palace, being extremely spoiled by him. Edward allowed the children to romp about in his presence in an abandoned way, kicking balls, playing catch. Their parents, the new Prince and Princess of Wales, had gone on a royal tour of the Empire. However, when Prince George and Princess Mary returned, they found their sons so undisciplined that they immediately appointed Frederick Finch as overall governor and Henry Hansell, son of a neighbouring Norfolk gentleman, as their tutor.

Hansell had previous experience as a royal schoolmaster and knew the form. Not aggressively academic, he played a reasonable game of golf and loved sailing. It was he who suggested to the Prince and Princess of Wales that the boys should go to a preparatory school. This idea was rejected out of hand as far too progressive, but Hansell tried to compensate by introducing companions for the boys. He organized cricket matches with boys from the local villages. But he was not always sympathetic. For instance, he insisted that Bertie should write with his right hand in the accepted way, although the child was clearly left-handed. (He

149

Prince Albert, the future George VI, with fellow naval cadets on board the Chippawa *at Niagara in June 1913*

played left-handed cricket and tennis and was good at both sports, playing at Wimbledon in the 1926 All-England Championships.) This prejudice added to his lack of assurance. His backwardness cut him off from his brother and sister Mary to whom he had been so attached as a small boy. And, to add to his shame and frustration, he was put into splints to cure his congenital condition of knock-knees. When he was thirteen he followed Edward to

Osborne to become a naval cadet, having failed to get in previously because of his atrocious maths. He was given a crash coaching course by a kindly tutor called Martin David and scraped through the exam, his best paper ironically being his French oral, stammer and all.

Even at this early age determination was a strong feature of his character. The sea-cadet school at Osborne was his first taste of a normal school life and it took him a year to settle in. He was a natural target for bullies despite his lineage, because of his stammer, his knees, his protruding ears (worse than Prince Charles's), and his desperate homesickness. Still, he made a few good friends whom he kept throughout his life and, though always bottom of the class, at least he was good at games. Bertie's academic record was not improved by a serious attack of whooping cough when he was fourteen, nor by the death of his beloved grandfather the following year.

The next hurdle was Dartmouth, again with a tough entrance exam. There were frequent family discussions on what would happen to poor Bertie if he did not get in. His father refused to believe his son should not get a place and in the event he was right. Bertie scraped in bottom of the list as usual. With extra maths coaching and extra engineering classes he managed, just, to keep afloat, but once again events beyond his control held him back. Hardly had he recovered from whooping cough than he got measles and the following year the Coronation took place with all the necessary and time-consuming preamble to the event. Dartmouth was even more of a normalizing influence than Osborne. Bertie's confidence grew. He even began to take part in schoolboy japes. He joined a gang of other cadets in driving a flock of sheep into a local dance hall and threatened to paint a new statue of his father red before its official unveiling.

The choice of education for any future little prince or princess is wide. Royal mothers in the last fifty years have sent their children away to a variety of schools. The most likely school for princes had been Eton before the Queen and Prince Philip sent Prince Charles to Gordonstoun. Royal girls' schools go in and out of fashion. Thirty years ago Heathfield in Ascot was *the* place. Princess

Alexandra was educated there, along with a gaggle of foreign princesses. A galaxy of ancillary preparatory schools sprang up in the surrounding area as a result. And then Heathfield declined in popularity. Too much socializing and not enough education, whispered prospective mothers. Then came Benenden whose old girls, reared on 'rats' bones' (corned beef) and Miss Cridland's lacrosse team, feature prominently in charity work and local government. Now the school that seems to be top of every royal mother's list, 'the only one I understand to which one's daughter should be sent', said Princess Michael of Kent, is St Mary's Wantage. St Mary's, until a few years ago, was run by Anglican nuns. It therefore had a convent atmosphere without the oppressive influence of Catholicism. Princess Alexandra and the Duchess of Kent both have daughters, Marina and Helen, at Wantage. Princess Alexandra is so serious about her daughter being treated like any other schoolgirl that she did not allow Marina to attend the Queen Mother's eightieth birthday celebrations because they came right in the middle of 'O' level revision.

St Mary's has an attitude to life less hearty than Benenden's and less snooty than Heathfield's. The school is equally capable of sending girls to Oxbridge as to the Royal Academy of Dramatic Art or the Royal College of Music.

'One is not wildly beefy at St Mary's Wantage,' said an old girl with several pounds of plums in her mouth. 'Of course, one's friends were very wealthy, but they didn't boast about it. I mean one could go through a whole school term without realizing that the girl in the bed next to you owned half of Scotland.'

St Mary's is on the edge of the Berkshire Downs in racing country. Every morning, as they get ready for morning chapel, the girls can see race-horses being ridden out from their stables in Lamborne and Newbury. Is it significant that the new headmistress used to teach at Gordonstoun?

Of the present Royal Family, Princess Michael, Austrian by birth and therefore not closely acquainted with the education system, private or public, in this country, makes a point of sounding out her friends and other royal mothers with school-age children for their opinions on the most suitable schools. When she first came to England as an eighteen-year-old student she was horrified at how badly educated the girls were compared to all the young men she knew. 'The girls knew nothing of art and music', said the Princess, 'but a lot about sport. They looked very healthy.' She was also surprised at the narrowness of their learning. Her idea of educating her children harks back to the time when it was thought essential for royal children to speak a lot of languages, and she would like her own children to grow up in a bilingual household. Princess Michael, not unexpectedly, speaks German as her first language.

Predictably, the most unconventional member of the present Royal Family, Princess Margaret, has chosen an unconventional school for her two children. Bedales, near Petersfield in Hampshire, is progressive, liberal, artistic, and co-educational. Dartington Hall and Frensham Heights are older schools in the same mould. Bedales is aggressively unsporty: there are token lacrosse matches with other schools, but pupils consider it *de rigueur* to lose. Team spirit is a low priority. The children are segregated only to sleep. The dormitories are in two buildings known as the Boys' Flat and the Girls' Flat. Peter Hall, Lord Olivier, and Cecil Day Lewis have all had children at Bedales. Drama and music come high on the curriculum. One year the school put on their version of Britten's *War Requiem* at Winchester Cathedral, an ambitious idea for an end-of-term school project.

Despite its emphasis an artistic pursuits, the academic standard of Bedales is high, but the school's real talent lies in its workshops. There are classes in jewellery, furniture-making, metal-work, and pottery. Viscount Linley is taking an advanced cabinet-making course and showing more than average skill. Bedales is self-consciously liberal and democratic in its outlook. There is no uniform, punk is the fashion, and though the teachers don't go overboard for green and purple striped hair, they tolerate it. Jeans and sweaters are the predominant dress for pupils and staff and the girls wear make-up; Lady Sarah experiments freely with silver-star eye-shadow.

However future royal babies may be educated, it seems that the width of the education will be more important than the depth. Above all, our twentieth-first-century royals must cultivate the social graces. They will be loved for their charm and self-assurance, not their 'A' levels.

The boy King, Richard II, enthroned in his coronation robes, holding the sceptre and orb

VI

Little Kings

Six little princes succeeded to the English throne before they had officially reached their majority – three Edwards, two Henrys, and one Richard. The legal majority of monarchs was something of a movable feast. Twenty-one was the official age, but in reality children matured earlier. Two of the child kings were married at fifteen and became fathers soon afterwards. At thirteen Henry III, dressed in a miniature suit of armour, was leading a splendid royal procession to the Scottish border for a summit meeting with Alexander II of Scotland, taking in the odd battle along the way. At fourteen Richard II showed remarkable precociousness in his handling of the Peasants' Revolt of 1381. And Edward VI, who came to the throne at nine already a brilliant scholar, showed powers of statesmanship far beyond his years. They would all in modern terms have been described as brats, but it was the brats who survived. Nice little boys like Edward V simply did not have the guile to last the course.

Only two little princesses became child queens, Victoria and Lady Jane Grey, the first at eighteen, the second at fifteen. Though strictly speaking Victoria had three years to run before she came of age there was never any doubt that from the first she was monarch in her own right with power to hire and fire, sign and seal, and God help anyone who dared to gainsay her. In this respect she does not fit comfortably into the category of child monarch. And as for poor Lady Jane, who was Queen of England for nine heady days, scarcely had she been proclaimed than she was kneeling before the executioner's block alongside her young husband, two pitiful pawns in the power struggle between rival factions. Nine days was not time enough for a coronation and hardly long enough for anyone without her winning ways to have made even a footnote in the history books.

The youngest English monarch was Henry VI, who inherited his father's throne at nine months. For child kings like him, ordinary coronation robes were too large and the little monarch had to be carried to the altar for the ceremony; the lengthy service had to be cut short for fear that the child would collapse and, as one would expect of nursery throne rooms, there was a deal of tears and beatings to punctuate the pomp and pageantry.

Where there are child kings there are always regents, protectors, and guardians. There were some good regents, but mostly they were an ambitious lot, either for themselves or for their relatives. Behind every boy king stands a long, impatient queue of pretenders, spurious claimants, potential usurpers. Bitter and often murderous feuds broke out between the monarch's relatives as each side tried to gain the supremacy. Henry III was lucky to have one of the few loyal protectors in the doubtful line of royal regents. William Marshal, Earl of Pembroke, had been appointed by the dying King John to mind his nine-year-old heir. It was not an easy job. John had left the kingdom in a mess; half of it was in the hands of French invaders, including London, which meant the new King had to be crowned at Gloucester. The country was so deeply divided that, in the interest of what modern politicians would call party unity, the coronation was organized with indecent haste and took place eleven days after John's death. Henry, who had been kept for safety in Devizes Castle, was despatched with his entourage to Gloucester meeting Marshal, his protector, at Malmesbury on the way. When the well-trained little lad saw Marshal, he bowed and doffed his cap and said, 'Welcome, sir. Truly I commit myself to God and to you that for God's sake you may take care of me and may the true God who takes care of all good things grant that you may so manage our business that your wardship of me may be prosperous.' He then burst into tears and everyone present followed suit.

There were other, more irritating hitches in the coronation proceedings. The Archbishop of Canterbury, who should have performed the ceremony, was in France at the time so the adaptable Marshal, a sort of Jack of all trades, stood proxy for Canterbury. Since the authentic crown was in London in the hands of the French, a makeshift crown was hastily prepared out of a chaplet belonging to Henry's mother Isabel of Angoulême. It looked more like a lady's hat than the royal crown of England. An observer described the child King as a pretty knight in his splendid coronation robes, but they were so heavy that the poor little boy couldn't walk under the weight and had to be carried home to change before heading on to the coronation banquet. His coronation oath, which he had learned by heart on the journey from Devizes, was that he would maintain honour, peace and, reverence due to God, his Church, and ordained ministers all his life, render right and justice to people committed to him, abolish bad laws and evil customs, observe good laws and customs, and make all do the same. He had also to pay homage to the Pope and Roman Catholic Church and continue to pay the Pontiff one thousand marks as promised by his father. All seemed to be going smoothly at the banquet until just after the third remove a messenger came tearing into the Great Hall with bad news. Goodrich Castle, not twelve miles from where the revellers were sitting, was being besieged by Louis of France's supporters. The diners dropped their roast capon drumsticks, seized their swords, and departed to do battle.

Eighteen months after the Gloucester coronation, Henry entered his capital city for the first time having made his peace with the French, the warring barons, and sundry other revolutionaries. Four years into his reign orders came from Rome and Pope Honorius III that he was to have a second coronation, using the right Archbishop and the proper crown. The Gloucester affair, said his Holiness, didn't count. By the time he was thirteen Henry was well ensconced in the duties of kingship. He made his royal progress north to confer with Alexander, the Scottish King, and, on his fourteenth birthday, was granted partial control over his kingdom independently of his protector. Popular opinion has it that, despite these precocious appearances, King Henry maintained the rather immature and narrow outlook of a schoolboy. He was prone to tantrums and though he never flew into rages like Henry II, who gnawed the rushes on the floor when worked up, he was always a little emotional.

Edward III was officially a minor when he came to the throne at fifteen, but no one could describe him as childlike. His father, the weak and ineffectual Edward II, had been persuaded to abdicate in his son's favour just two weeks after his son's coronation at Westminster. Edward II died in hideous circumstances in the dungeons of Berkeley Castle in Gloucestershire. Edward III was well up to coping with the rivalries between his mother's ambitious lover Roger de Mortimer and the equally ambitious Henry of Lancaster. At sixteen he married Philippa of Hainault and a year later their eldest son, the Black Prince, was born. All this when Edward was still officially a minor, but there was more adventure to come. When he was eighteen Edward routed Mortimer and his supporters. Mortimer was executed and Edward's mother imprisoned; the King had at last proved his ability to reign single-handed.

The untimely death of the Black Prince was the cue for the next child monarch to make his entrance on the historical stage. Richard II came to the throne at the age of ten. Throughout his minority the enigmatic and slightly sinister figure of his Machiavellian uncle, John of Gaunt, lay like a dark shadow across the land. Gaunt was always suspected of ulterior motives, despite his professed loyalty to the Crown. The forty years up to Richard's accession are littered with intermittent warfare, both at home and abroad, resulting in a host of private armies that could easily be used against a weak child king. Richard's coronation was organized by his uncle Gaunt. It was an impressive affair designed to emphasize the sanctity and magnificence of hereditary monarchy and to usher in, it was hoped, a new period of harmony. France had other ideas and celebrated Richard's coronation by raiding the English coast. The greatest influence on Richard's early life was his beautiful, gentle, thrice-married mother, Joan. His tutor Robert Birley was another benign soul, but neither his mother nor Birley was any match for the Earls of Oxford, Arundel, Gloucester, and Warwick, all lusting for power.

In 1381, when he was just fourteen, Richard met his greatest challenge in the Peasants' Revolt led by Wat Tyler. The young King was shut up in the Tower for safety with his councillors as the peasants marched upon London and from a garret window he watched his city go up in flames. He was not actually in danger, for the watchword of the rebels was 'King Richard and a true Commons', but with Gaunt in Scotland and most of the army

158

fighting either in Wales or in France it was little wonder that the boy should feel apprehensive. Still, he came good, rising to the occasion by riding out to Mile End to meet the rebels. Wat Tyler spoke to the young King, asking him to grant the abolition of serfdom, a fixed low rent for all land, and an amnesty for the rebels. Richard agreed, but there remained a hard core of the peasant rebels who refused to accept the new peace terms. The boy King had a second meeting with Tyler which proved to be the more dramatic. Tyler rode out to meet him with further demands and was seized in a planned ambush by the King's men and summarily executed. The peasants behind Tyler began to string their bows menacingly, but Richard with great, and probably foolhardy, courage rode out alone towards them saying, 'Sirs, will you kill your King? I am your King. I am your captain and your leader. Follow me into the fields,' whereupon, with a fine line in exits, he turned about and rode into the fields of St John's Clerkenwell. The peasants followed cheering.

Tyler's death signalled the end of the revolt in London and it gradually died down elsewhere. It gave the King's reputation a huge and much needed fillip and taught him two invaluable lessons in statecraft: first, the power of deceit in dispensing with trouble (the original Mile End demands had never been granted); second, it alerted Richard to the almost mystical faith that the rebels had in their King, which was later to allow the grown man to have almost mystical faith in his own ability to rule.

The year after the Peasants' Revolt, when he was fifteen, Richard married Anne of Bohemia. He was at the time of his marriage a sophisticated, worldly, intelligent, foppish youth, a connoisseur of art, literature, and music with a flair for colourful and fashionable dress. He was emotional, introspective, complicated, romantic. His favourite reading included twelve French romances, one about King Arthur, another about Percival and Gawain, *The Romance of the Rose*, and a book of lays. He composed songs, lays, ballads, and roundels and sang in services in his own chapel to his own musical compositions. He was also devoted to the memory of Edward II and beavered to promote his canonization; Birley had grounded him well in the principles of royalty. On a less elevated level he introduced the handkerchief to the Great British Wardrobe. His tailor specified in detail the supply of 'little pieces for giving to the Lord King for carrying in his hand to wipe and cleanse his nose'. Until his official coming of age at twenty-one, Richard's reign was clouded with internecine quarrels and eventually he was forced, like his beloved great-grandfather, to abdicate.

Henry vi, the baby King, inherited along with his kingdom the memory of his great father Henry v who died campaigning at Vincennes in France in September 1422. He had a lot to live up to: a father who was known as 'the flower of Christian chivalry', the victor of Agincourt, conqueror of Normandy, and heir and Regent to the kingdom of France. On 28 September 1422 the Bishop of Durham delivered the Great Seal into the small, podgy hands of the baby King in the presence of the Lords. The instrument of authority was then committed to a temporary keeper. There is no suggestion in the records that the circumstances surrounding Henry's accession were anything other than normal; no mention of swaddling or teething, no talk of tantrums, no hint that the King was not fully responsible and an adult monarch in charge of his administration. All official documents were always issued in the name of *Henricus Dei Gratia Rex Angliae et Franciae et Dominus Hiberniae.* Councillors drew their authority from 'his' letters of commission and subjects addressed petitions to the King.

Within two months of Henry becoming King of England, Charles vi of France died and hence Henry was also King of France, still short of his first birthday. His uncles and cousins did most of the ruling for the first twenty years of his reign, obviously keen to take advantage of new opportunities presented by a weak monarch in the aftermath of the strong and powerful Henry v. Baby Henry was paraded in public amidst great ceremony from a very early age, either seated on his mother's lap or tottering on his own two feet behind his royal relatives. He saw less and less of his mother Katherine of France as he grew up, for she had moved in with a Welsh squire, Owen Tudor, and was consequently too busy raising a second family to have much time for her regal son. This lack of a real mother was to have a huge effect on the child. He grew up to be aloof, repressed, and unable to form deep friendships. When he was in the care of Richard Beauchamp, Earl of Warwick, he was a precocious child and, at the age of ten, was asking his governor whether he, a King, should be chastised for his misdemeanours. The answer came plainly enough. Warwick thrashed him the harder for his impertinence.

He had every right to be precocious, for he was introduced to the most intractable problems of his reign at an early age. There was, for a start, the deteriorating situation in France caused by a tiresome young woman called Joan of Arc leading the Valois revival. The Regent in France, Henry's uncle, John Duke of Bedford, was worried enough about the situation there to call for his nephew's coronation in Paris. Hence on 2 December 1431 Henry was crowned in Paris at St Denis, a lavish spectacle featuring four hundred plumed horses and a military cavalcade three miles away. However, it was not to last for long. The Duke of Burgundy made a separate alliance with Henry's enemies and the trusty Bedford died in 1435. Henry, aged fourteen, burst into tears when he received the letter from Burgundy telling of his defection, because the letter was only addressed to the King of England and not of France as well. Although his French sovereignty did not last long, at least he had the distinction of being the only English monarch to be crowned in both England and France.

Henry had had a lot of exposure to the ceremony of government as a child. When he was three he was brought to open Parliament and 'shriked and cryed and sprang; and he was then led upon his feet to the choir of St Paul's by the Lord Protector and the Duke of Exeter, and afterwards set upon a fair courser and conveyed through Chepe'. Another uncle, Humphrey, Duke of Gloucester had been named as Regent in Henry v's will, but he was a poor statesman and distrusted by his peers. They dismissed him saying that Henry was to have a Council to rule for him rather than a Regent. Humphrey was always scrapping with another of the King's relatives, and pillar of the Lancastrian establishment, Cardinal Beaufort. At an early age Henry learned domestic diplomacy. He would try and mediate between the two crabby, jealous men by saying that both were innocent of blame and just as good as each other. The Council saw Henry safely through until around 1436, when he was fifteen. There is no official documentation as to the precise date, but Warwick was relieved of his duties as tutor in May 1436 and by January 1437 the office of the King was firmly established. Although to us fifteen seems a young age to end the minority Henry vi's father had been the same age when he was put in charge of military operations against the Welsh rebels.

Henry was never really a child, partly because of his early

161

Here foloweth howe according to the last voice of kyng Hen̄r̄ie 6th Erle Richard
by the auctorite of the hole pliament was maistre to kyng Hem the 6th And
so he contenued til the kyng was ...... yere of age And then cast by
his greet labour he was discharged

Richard Beauchamp, Earl of Warwick, being made master of the infant King,
Henry VI

Henry VI being crowned King of England in Westminster Abbey on 6 November 1429. Two years later, he was also crowned King of France in Paris: the only English monarch to receive both crowns

succession, but mainly because of the departure of his mother to the Tudor household. From an early age he dressed in black and took no interest in fashion. When he had to wear a crown on feast days he would also wear a hair shirt next to his skin to compensate for the frivolity. At sixteen he used a wooden stamp of his signature, one of the first of its kind which had been originally made for him as a toy. He didn't, on the whole, go in for orthodox toys like the cup and ball or soldiers. Instead he preferred spying on his servants 'through hidden windows of his chamber, to see if any foolish women had come into the household to corrupt his staff'. He was not a very lovable child.

The saddest little king never to be crowned was Edward v. He was such a pretty fellow, all golden curls and pink cheeks, with the sort of face that shines out from Christmas cards under a holly branch singing carols in a clean white surplice. The contemporary diarist Mancini described him at the age of ten, two years before he was proclaimed King, as having 'such dignity in his whole person, and in his face such charm that the beholders were never tired of looking at him'.

Edward, elder of the two pathetic Princes in the Tower, was doomed from the start to be a victim. Throughout his short life the shadow of the Wars of the Roses hung over his chances and his future. Unwittingly, his father Edward iv had appointed his own younger brother Richard, Duke of Gloucester, to be his son's Protector in the event of his own death and it was to be Richard who would prove the most treacherous of all the little Prince's adversaries. Edward v's reign lasted only two months. During that time he ostensibly held the reins of sovereignty, signing letters of State and sealing them with the Great Seal of England, but in truth the dark figure of his unscrupulous, hunchback uncle was the real power behind the throne.

Theoretically, Edward should have been well-trained to deal with the intrigues that were continually being hatched in and around the corridors of the court, for this was the period *par excellence* of nefarious wheeling and dealing for power. But most of his childhood had been spent in the comparative tranquillity of Ludlow Castle, as befitted the little Prince of Wales, with his younger brother Richard. Here, under the tutelage of his beloved uncle Anthony Woodville. Earl Rivers, he had studied, played and gained a reputation for being a clever, quiet, studious boy

164

who could discourse elegantly and fully understand and recite by heart just about any piece of literature, either in verse or prose, that came into his hands, provided the author were not too abstruse. When his father died, his mother Elizabeth Woodville, rightly fearing that her brother-in-law the Duke of Gloucester would try to seize power, lost no time in setting the coronation date for her son, the popular assumption being that a crowned king was a great deal harder to dethrone than an uncrowned one. The coronation date was set for a couple of months thence, at the end of June 1483.

Even before the new King's entourage had left Ludlow for London the coronation robes had been ordered, a long and a short one for Edward, the first in cloth of gold, the second in purple with a long train lined with white damask. The household account books also mention other suits of State for the little King, like the blue velvet riding habit with black damask doublet and sleeves which he wore on his triumphant arrival into London. His hench-men had matching suits with embroidered hoods.

Almost from the start things began to go badly wrong. Uncle Richard intercepted the royal party, Edward's beloved maternal uncle, Rivers, was arrested on trumped-up charges, and the child's black-hearted Protector took charge of the progress. Their arrival in London from the north reads like something from the scenario of a Hollywood melodrama. Surrounded by cheering crowds the beautiful little King, dressed in his blue velvet habit, his fair curls hanging about his shoulders, was officially presented to the Bishop of London in Hackney Fields. The Bishop's household were dressed in scarlet, the King's in purple and, appropriately, the Duke of Gloucester was clad exclusively in black. Outwardly, Richard was behaving exactly as a devoted uncle should. He made much of presenting his nephew to the crowd crying 'Behold the King', no doubt trying to allay the boy's fears about the fate of Earl Rivers.

The next problem was where to house the royal party. The Dowager Queen, hearing of her brother Anthony's arrest, had acted promptly and together with her other children, her household, and as much silver, plate, and jewels as she could conveniently take with her, she had sought sanctuary with the Abbot of Westminster. The obvious place for the King and his entourage to stay was the Palace of Westminster, but this was too

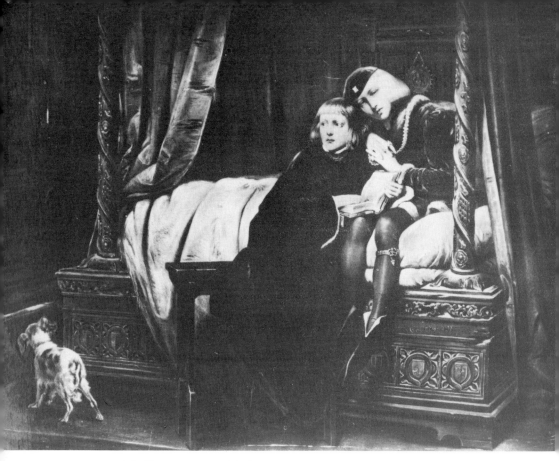

The Victorian image of the Princes in the Tower – Edward V and Richard, Duke of York

near his rebellious mother for Gloucester's comfort, so once again the Protector took charge and despatched the whole crew to the royal apartments in the Tower of London. He also persuaded the Dowager Queen and the Abbot of Westminster to let Edward's younger brother, Richard, Duke of York, join the King in the Tower.

There is a sinister entry in the accounts for the Tower at that time which specifies that on 21 May 1483, a few days before Edward arrived in his new quarters, six carpenters were hired for one day at a cost of threepence per man to make certain alterations therein. There is also a record of three beds being built and payment for one hundred and a quarter feet of board, two sacks of lime, and a quantity of nails – provisions more suited to a prison than a palace.

Whatever his wicked uncle's instructions to those mysterious carpenters, Edward was not at this stage at least treated like a prisoner. All the official business of State, the letters patent, the despatches from foreign envoys, petitions, and other State paraphernalia were brought to the Tower for the twelve-year-old sovereign to sign. One of the first papers that he put his name to was a petition from the Abbess of Shaftesbury, in which she sought the royal approval for two prospective novices, Mistress Elizabeth and Mistress Lucy. But even while this apparent normality was taking place, the scheming Richard was setting about feathering his own nest. Insidiously at first, but increasingly with more openness, he was spreading the rumour that the King and his younger brother wre illegitimate because Edward iv had been betrothed to another before his marriage to Elizabeth Woodville. Under canon law this meant that any children from the Woodville marriage were bastards. Anyone who spoke up against the illegitimacy claim was arrested and disposed of and, finally, the Council pronounced in the Duke of Gloucester's favour and proclaimed him rightful King. Overnight Edward v's status changed. He was no longer the King, but the Lord Bastard. When the news of his uncle's treachery was broken to him in the Tower he said, sadly, 'Alas, I would my uncle would let me have my life yet though I lose my kingdom'. Wishful thinking.

King Richard was crowned with due pomp and ceremony, rather more in fact than usual. The King, clad in cloth of gold and a long purple train, walked under a canopy held by the wardens of the Cinque Ports. He and his Queen then walked barefoot over a crimson carpet from Westminster Palace to the Abbey to be anointed. Richard gave solemn public assurances that no harm would befall his nephew, but after the autumn of that year the little Princes, who previously had been seen walking in the Tower gardens playing with balls and sticks, were never seen alive again. How active a role Richard played in their deaths is open to speculation. So also is the method of their murder. Were they smothered, strangled, stabbed, or just, as seems more likely, neglected and left to die without food, air or affection? Two hundred years later the bones of two children were discovered in the walls of an upper room at the Tower. Medical examination showed that the elder child had been four feet ten inches, the younger four feet six and a half inches and the fingers were very,

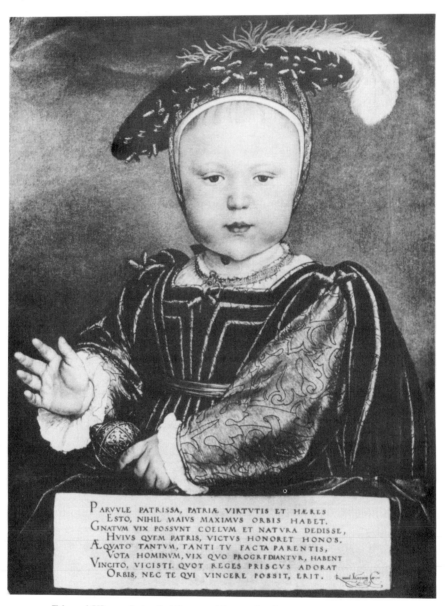

PARVVLE PATRISSA, PATRIÆ VIRTVTIS ET HÆRES
  ESTO, NIHIL MAIVS MAXIMVS ORBIS HABET.
GNATVM VIX POSSVNT COELVM ET NATVRA DEDISSE,
  HVIVS QVEM PATRIS, VICTVS HONORET HONOS.
ÆQVATO TANTVM, TANTI TV FACTA PARENTIS,
  VOTA HOMINVM, VIX QVO PROGREDIANTVR, HABENT
VINCITO, VICISTI. QVOT REGES PRISCVS ADORAT
  ORBIS, NEC TE QVI VINCERE POSSIT, ERIT.

Edward VI as a baby, holding a golden rattle, from a portrait by Holbein very small – a fittingly poignant testament to one of the darker incidents in English history.

The last child king was Edward VI. His father, Henry VIII, died on 28 January 1547, in the belief that he had made careful constitutional arrangements for his son's minority. But he had reckoned without Edward's uncle, Edward Seymour, Earl of Hertford (and subsequently Duke of Somerset), who seized effective power by overturning the Council of Regency and establishing himself as Protector of the Realm and guardian of the boy King. From then until Somerset's downfall, Edward was a puppet of Somerset and his faction.

Edward's coronation was a lavish affair, even by extravagant Tudor standards. His procession started at the Tower, continued past St Mary-le-Bow Church in Cheapside, skirted the old St Paul's, and progressed down the Strand to Westminster. The pale, serious-looking monarch, all of nine years old, was in magnanimous mood. He created forty Knights of the Bath (including five of his old playmates) and fifty-five Knights of the Garter after the ceremony. He was crowned with the Crown of St Edward by his godfather, Thomas Cranmer, Archbishop of Canterbury, his father's old ally in his battle with the Pope and the Catholic loyalists at home. The streets were hung with gold tapestries, flags, and streamers. As the procession streamed to Westminster, Edward reined in his horse to hear children singing his praises and to watch pageants and musical tableaux put on for the occasion. The Mayor of London gave him a purse of one thousand crowns according to custom, but it was too heavy for the child to carry. He took four hours to get from the Tower to Westminster with so many distractions along the way. Because he was so young, the coronation ceremony was cut from twelve hours to seven. The banquet afterwards lasted a further four hours and each course was brought in to the sound of trumpets and preceded by two noblemen on horseback. Edward sat between his god-father, the Archbishop of Canterbury, and the Duke of Somerset. It was more of a State stag party, because there were no women present, by tradition, either at the coronation or the banquet.

Naturally Edward, the greatest royal scholar, continued to study during his minority and by the time he was thirteen had read Aristotle's *Ethics* in the Greek original and had translated Cicero's *De Philosophia* from Latin into Greek. He was *clavis regni* (key to the kingdom) from the beginning of his minority and hence he was constantly the target for people trying to win his favour. For instance, Thomas Seymour, the Lord Admiral and Somerset's younger brother, had aspirations to power and got on well with Edward. He married the Queen Dowager (Catherine Parr) and tried to bribe his new step-son with pocket money; Somerset was very mean when it came to doling out spending money to the King. But Seymour and his hand-outs overstepped the mark. Edward was awoken one night by the sound of his pet dog barking outside his bedroom door. This was followed by a pistol shot and Seymour was caught red-handed with a still-smoking pistol having killed the wretched animal. His excuse was that he was checking to see if the King was well-guarded, but it was pretty lame at best and not sufficient to prevent him being packed off, despite his lofty status, to the Tower on charges of treason and conspiracy.

It was at his trial after Queen Catherine's death that Thomas Seymour's ultimate plan was revealed: to marry Elizabeth, Edward's step-sister, kill Edward, and become king. He was, of course, executed. Elizabeth was put under much scrutiny, but nothing could be proved against her. She seemed to be everything a doting, elder sister should be to the little King. She sewed shirts and wrote amusing letters in Latin to her little half-brother; whereas Mary remained aloof from court. Edward got his own back on the latter by writing treatises against the Pope's supremacy, which he dedicated to his Regent, Somerset.

But despite the intrigues and plots Edward, the boy King, played and larked about with his friends and, in particular, his Irish chum Barnaby Fitzpatrick. He was also waited on hand and foot with one servant to remove his shoes and another his stockings. His bed was always searched by a guard of yeomen before he got into it in case an assassin should be lurking behind the arras or between the sheets. His step-mother, Queen Catherine, was kept at arm's length by Somerset, who also discouraged intimacy with his sister Elizabeth. When Queen Catherine died in childbirth in 1548 Edward showed no emotion. Indeed, he was a cold fish by nature. He was unmoved by the news of Thomas Seymour's execution and even when Somerset eventually fell foul of his own plots and met the same end, Edward did not weep. In truth, Somerset was always very domineering with Edward, making the King feel more like his manservant than His Majesty.

Ever since the dead-dog-at-the-bedchamber incident Somerset had slept next door to Edward. Somerset's downfall was the stuff that *Boy's Own* adventure stories are made of. Five hundred men attacked Hampton Court one night, bent on murdering the Protector. Edward and Somerset escaped to the more secure ramparts of Windsor Castle. Edward, then aged twelve, armed himself with a jewelled dagger that his father had given him and was greeted outside the castle by supportive crowds; but Somerset knew the game was up. The King's army was backing his enemies, led by John Dudley, Lord Warwick. Edward received them at Windsor three days later, to be told that Somerset was a traitor who had enriched himself with the Crown's wealth. Somerset confessed to all his charges and begged on his knees for his life. When he rose to his feet the King graciously granted it, but Somerset was relieved of his property – all his movables, vast tracts of lands, and two hundred manors. He made a last vain attempt to regain power which led to his eventual, complete downfall and execution. Edward recorded the affair in his journal, showing that by this time (1551) at the age of fourteen he was perfectly capable of making independent judgements.

John Dudley, who became Duke of Northumberland, was now in power and he wisely encouraged Edward to participate in affairs of State, as a means of ensuring the King's support. Royal prerogative was gradually becoming a reality rather than merely a token gesture.

On the day before his fourteenth birthday Edward took great pleasure in knighting his beloved tutor John Cheke and his friend, Henry Sidney, who was to be permanently at his side during his fatal illness. When he was fifteen Edward was betrothed to the King of France's eldest daughter Isabelle, but it was at that time he first began to be ill. The royal progress of that summer tired him tremendously, but even when he was in bed seriously ill he insisted on seeing his councillors every day. He was too weak to open Parliament, so Parliament went to him at Whitehall. He wore a crimson train ten yards long and sat in a State chair signing acts hour after hour. In the last weeks of his life, he changed the succession in favour of the Protestant Lady Jane Grey rather than his virulently Catholic sister, Mary. On the night of his death, which was slow, painful, and probably worsened by the quack remedies he had been given, a tremendous thunderstorm broke over London washing away bridges and a church spire – a fitting omen for the severity of the reign of his sister Bloody Mary that was to come.

VII

The Family Way

The keynote of royal upbringing ever since George III, Queen Charlotte and their surviving brood of thirteen has been the emphasis on family life. Queen Charlotte liked nothing better than to be surrounded by her children, whether she was dreaming up new apple-pudding recipes to use up stale bread, or walking by the river at their home in Kew, with the boys sailing home-made boats and the girls bowling hoops. King George, who was notoriously thrifty, insisted that the children eat porridge every morning because it was cheap as well as substantial and always laid and lit the fire himself to make sure no firewood was wasted. Sometimes he allowed the elder princes to help him. Their home was conspicuously child-orientated, with special low hooks for the little princesses to hang their hooped petticoats on at night.

But it was the home life of Victoria and Albert that really set the seal on the importance of a happy family even though, ironically, not all its members were happy. Though Prince Albert was a strict father, he was also an adoring one, taking endless pains over his children's upbringing. Bertie's tutor, Mr Birch, had to report daily on his pupil's progress (or lack of it) and when Princess Vicky, Albert's eldest and favourite daughter, became engaged to Fritz, the Crown Prince of Prussia, he set aside two hours of his already crammed day expressly to instruct her as to how she should conduct herself socially, officially and privately as the consort of a foreign monarch. He, after all, was in a good position to give advice.

173

Queen Charlotte with her two eldest sons: George, Prince of Wales, later George IV, stands holding a bow, while Frederick, Duke of York, sits on her lap. On the piano lies a copy of Some Thoughts concerning Education *by John Locke – not enough thoughts were applied to the education of these two princes, however, for they grew up to drink openly in the schoolroom and to terrify their tutors*

Victoria's family is a perfect example of what bringing up royal children was, is, and always has been about – the strange and unnatural contrast between private informality and public formality which must have been confusing for a young child. Bertie experienced this curious dichotomy when he went on his first sea cruise with his parents along the Cornish coast. Everywhere the ship anchored the little Prince was fêted and fussed over. The Captain sent messages which read 'God Bless Our Little Admiral'. But as soon as he was back below deck he was once more under the thumb of strict governors, tutors, and scolding nannies – an ordinary little boy again.

Modern royal children, with their more casual life style, have less difficulty working out their identities. Their lives, after all, are not so very different from those of children in any well-heeled, upper-class home where second cars, country houses, foreign holidays and boarding schools are taken for granted. Princess Anne said recently on television that she doubted that her children would even *feel* royal, and she certainly does not intend to give them any royal titles. Peter and Zara Phillips lead a typical landed-gentry country life with bicycles in the garage, ponies in the stables and weekend outings to the local gymkhanas, where more than likely they will see both their parents taking part in the events. Whenever she is not on duty, Princess Anne likes to put on a plastic apron, roll up her sleeves and head up to the nursery wing at Gatcombe Park to give the children their baths, read them bedtime stories, administer positively last mugs of cocoa, and tuck them up for the night.

In the Queen's private rooms at Buckingham Palace there is a small kitchen where, on a free evening, she will happily potter, making herself a cup of instant coffee and a slice of toast. And if Prince Edward happens to be at home from school, they will both sit with scrambled eggs on trays on their laps in front of the television in her comfortable, chintzy, private sitting-room.

Being royal at boarding school does not entail any special privileges. It used to be otherwise. When Prince Henry, Duke of Gloucester went to Eton, his father got special dispensation for him to skip Latin and concentrate on French and German because, said the Prince of Wales, the future George v, they would be more useful to him. And a generation earlier he himself as a naval cadet on his first long sea voyage had been excused the

'Windsor Castle in Modern Times', a portrayal of the home life of Victoria and Albert, painted by Sir Edwin Landseer in 1842. While Vicky, the Princess Royal, plays with the terriers and her father's hunting bag, the Queen's mother, the Duchess of Kent, can just be seen in the garden, wheeling Albert Edward, the Prince of Wales, in a pram

Night Watch on the grounds, said his father Edward vii, that his health would not allow it. But modern royals are not so molly-coddled. Princess Anne at Benenden ate her share of 'rats' bones', 'dead man's leg' (steamed jam roll), and 'Ganges mud' (chocolate blancmange).

There are times, of course, when having a handle to your name can smooth your path. When your father is President of the Football Association, there is no necessity to queue for Cup Final tickets, as twelve-year-old Nicholas Windsor, elder son of the

Duke of Kent, discovered. Sitting next to the Duke at Wembley for his first F.A. Cup Final, he was asked at half-time what he would like by way of refreshment. 'Champagne, please,' he said.

But four hundred years ago, royal children accepted formality as part of even the most mundane exercises. Take bedmaking. Most of the young royals today have continental quilts (along with their continental mothers), which they throw over their beds in a trice. But little Henry Tudor, son of Henry VII, would have had a very different concept of how to make a bed, having seen the palaver and the man-power involved in making his father's four-poster in the Painted Chamber of Westminster Palace. It was an undertaking only slightly less complicated than the Sun King's *Grande Levée*. Every evening ten men with appropriately official titles sallied forth to do their royal duty in the King's bedroom. The production began with the Groom of the Bedchamber summoning with trumpets four Yeomen of the Wardrobe who brought in the sheets and blankets. Hard on their heels came four Yeomen of the Bedchamber and a Gentleman Usher who was in Supreme Command. The Groom would then stand at the foot of the bed holding aloft a lighted torch while four Yeomen lined up on each side of the bed. One of them would scrabble about in the straw of the bed with a dagger prodding and jabbing to make certain 'there be no untruth therein' (such as an intruder bent on regicide who might have slipped in with the warming-pan) after which a canvas cloth was thrown over the straw and on top of this a feather mattress which had been hanging up to air. With the mattress in position another Yeoman, roughly the same size and weight as the monarch, would lie on the mattress and roll about testing it to see that there were no uncomfortable lumps or bumps and that the feathers and underlying straw were evenly distributed. Satisfied that the surface was smooth, the Groom would bark out another order whereupon the eight Yeomen in a time-honoured ritual would put on the sheets, taking care that their eight pairs of hands worked together so that the huge sheet touched the mattress at all points at the same moment. Heaven help the Yeoman who got it wrong. When all the bedding was safely in place each bedmaker made a sign of the cross and kissed that part of the bed that his hands had touched. The Groom drew the curtains round the bed and a page was left to keep vigil until Henry returned for the night. With this kind of carry-on an everyday occurrence, Tudor children quickly learned the importance of ceremonials and how to conduct themselves therein. As a solemn eight-year-old Prince Henry, in the absence of his father, entertained Thomas More and Erasmus to dinner under the wonderful hammer-beamed ceiling of the Great Hall at Eltham Palace.

Royal households have dwindled over the years. Where ten men made Henry VII's bed one, or at most two, chambermaids take care of the beds at Buckingham Palace. The younger members of the family make their own. But there was no shortage of staff in the household of Charles I's sister, Princess Mary, whose domestic work-force consisted of three grooms, nine ladies of the bedchamber, a gentleman usher, several warders, two pages, four footmen, five kitchen servants, a coachman, a groom (the stables alone cost £6,000 a year to run) various seamstresses, laundresses, and a French apothecary (who didn't get paid for the medicines he prescribed but made up for it by charging through the nose for odoriforous waters, powders, and perfumes). The Hanoverians also kept a large number of servants. Queen Charlotte's tribe was divided into groups according to age and sex to make it easier for their nursemaids to control them. But though Victoria's nursery bristled with nursery-maids and seamstresses, the atmosphere, once the tyrannical Baroness Lehzen had been sacked and sent back to Germany by the Prince Consort (this caused Victoria and Albert's first marital tiff), was much less stuffy. The main reason for this was the presence of Lady Lyttleton who was in charge of the royal nursery. She was herself a devoted mother and the sort of woman to whom children instinctively turned for comfort. It was just as well that they had her, for the Queen, their own mother, made no bones about the fact that she found small children tiresome, unattractive, and tedious.

'An ugly baby' wrote the Queen in her usual forthright manner, 'is a very nasty object and the prettiest is frightful when undressed – in short, as long as they have their big body and little limbs and that terrible frog-like action.' Of her youngest son, Prince Leopold, the sickliest of the family who suffered from the family's curse of haemophilia, she wrote when he was four years old, 'He is tall but holds himself worse than ever and is a very common looking child – very plain of face, clever but an oddity – and not an engaging child though amusing.' Victoria was more than happy to turn the nursery over to Albert and Lady Lyttleton. Albert, being very German, advocated sunny rooms with lots of fresh air and open windows at night, even in mid-winter, and insisted his children be vaccinated – a very modern idea. He also preached thrift. The ribbons that trimmed his wife's old hats had to be unpicked and used again to trim his daughters' dresses. Nursery food was very plain. 'It was quite a poor living, only a bit of roast meat and perhaps plain pudding,' recalled one of the royal nursery-maids, Miss Jane Jones. As for Victoria's grandchildren, their tastes were even simpler. There was nothing that the children of Bertie, Prince of Wales, liked better than toast, and their father had a favourite game of letting them race pieces of buttered toast down his trouser leg.

For Victoria's children, life was undoubtedly sheltered. William the Conqueror's children, by contrast, played with real daggers and jumped from real castle walls, fighting real enemies when they were barely in their teens. Children in the Middle Ages matured earlier, married earlier, and in many cases died earlier. They were used to experiencing such unchildlike things as war, public executions and mutilations, and would be taken to bear-baiting and cock-fighting sessions for entertainment.

Even in the 'enlightened' seventeenth century, dwarfs and hunchbacks were indispensable members of the court. Queen Henrietta Maria was enchanted when, out of a large raised pie that had just been cut open on the table before her, there stepped a tiny little figure barely two feet high who prostrated himself on the tablecloth before her and begged to be taken into royal service. His name, he said, was Geoffrey Dawson and he came from a reputable family. The Queen (who was no more than four feet four inches herself) was so tickled at this bizarre application for work that she hired him on the spot and despatched him immediately to France to fetch her accoucheur, for she was expecting her first baby. Mr Dawson went to Paris, collected the accoucheur, and headed home, bearing gifts from the Queen's French relatives. But in the Channel their ship was captured by privateers and held to ransom for more than a year. To us this may seem a tall story, but to Henrietta Maria's children who grew up with such curiosities about them, it would not have been so strange. Dwarfs were a feature of court life. James II's two daughters, Mary and Anne, were taught to draw and paint by a famous art master

179

called Richard Gibson who was no more than three feet ten inches, his wife was even smaller.

In other ways, too, there were exotic times. Witness the extravagant banquets to which John of Gaunt took his nephew, Richard II, as a lad. At Tattersall Castle in Lincoln the table groaned with twelve hundred roasted pigeons and eleven thousand pigeons eggs as well as sundry other cuts of game, fowl, pies, and puddings. The second floor of the south-east tower at Tattersall was given over to breeding pigeons expressly for the table. Richard was used to feasts that were marathon and rich, for they were the order of the day. Medieval palates were not satisfied by bland food as any early cookery book will prove. Into the pot went the goose, the swan, the figs, the honey, the spices, the herbs, the scallions (a kind of onion), the almonds, the cream, the oysters, the ale, and the wine. The main meal of the day in noble households started at about eleven in the morning and could last for four or five hours, with entertainments punctuating the courses. Harp players, lute players, poets, jugglers, and acrobats were all part of the bill of fare and during one Norman banquet it is recorded that a troubadour recited five thousand lines of verse between the removes, which must have made the little princes and princesses at the lower tables, patiently waiting for their pudding, extremely restive.

Children have always had a sweet tooth and cakes and puddings have played an important role in their diet. Queen Charlotte gave her children greengage tart and Victoria's children were particularly partial to gingerbread. It was a universal craving. No Victorian fair would have been complete without a gingerbread stall. We come down to earth with a bump to hear that Prince Charles's favourite meal as a child was boiled chicken and rice pudding. He has not changed much since then and, although the Princess of Wales went through the statutory cookery course that all well-brought-up young ladies complete these days, she too prefers plain roast meals with perhaps a bar of chocolate to finish off.

It was not merely the size of the staff in royal households that dwindles as we approach the present day, but also the size of the families themselves. Queen Victoria's was the last really large royal family and though the present Princess of Wales has often said she would adore to have at least six children, the average number of royal children per family these days is hardly more than three. Small families, even though there may be dozens of cousins and second cousins lurking in neighbouring shires, bring other problems, for children, whether royal or otherwise, need play-fellows. Queen Victoria did not believe in importing friends to play with her children. 'I have a great fear' she once said, 'of young and carefully brought-up boys mixing with older boys and indeed with any boys in general, for the mischief done by bad boys and the things they may hear and learn from them cannot be over-rated.' Fortunately her carefully brought-up sons had siblings enough to play with and ironically, despite their careful upbringing, they did not turn out to be paragons of virtue, any of them.

There is little doubt that children from large families have a more relaxed and tolerant attitude to life, for they have had to learn from the earliest age how to share their toys, their time, and their affections. Medieval royal children were never short of playmates, for the households of aristocratic and royal families were invariably swollen in number by little orphans whose fathers had been killed in battle and mothers who had died in childbirth, The head of the family took them in as wards and would be able to exploit their lands during their minority and marry them off for political ends. These children would live on equal terms with the real children of the house, sharing their schoolroom, their playthings and their beds.

It is only recently that royal parents have again allowed their children to mix freely with commoners. Compared to her own four children, the Queen had a very isolated childhood with her younger sister Margaret. Although they lived in the very heart of London, at 145 Piccadilly, and made frequent sorties to Hyde Park with their governess, Marion Crawford, they were not allowed to play with the other children there. It sounds rather a lonely childhood for the little Princesses, despite their doting parents and adoring grandparents. Every morning when she woke up, Lillibet would run to the window which faced south over

The vast progeny of Victoria and Albert. The Queen is shown with her children, grandchildren and great-grandchildren including most of the crowned heads of Europe – celebrating her Golden Jubilee in 1887

The little Princesses, Elizabeth and Margaret Rose, in 1933

Green Park towards Buckingham Palace to wave to grandfather, who would be looking out for her from his own room flourishing a white handkerchief. They had everything they wanted but young companions, which is probably why the Queen chose to send her own children away to boarding schools where they would lead a normal life surrounded by children of their own age.

One aspect of life that has remained constant over the centuries is the way that royal princes and princesses have enjoyed themselves. Take the giving and receiving of presents, for instance. Little Mary Tudor was given a rosemary bush spangled with tinsel and jewels by her parents as a birthday present, while, according to the account books, she gave her sister Princess Elizabeth a pair of singing birds, pretty painted shoes, some flowers, and, rather mysteriously, 'greyhounds'. Edward III's daughter was given on her birthday a live hare with a jewelled collar, while Princess Margaret, rather more prosaically, was presented with a series of farm animals from Woolworths, lined up on the table in the nursery at the Royal Lodge Windsor on her first birthday.

Victoria's family, from Albert Edward down to baby Beatrice, were inordinately fond of celebrating special occasions and naturally these occasions, as in all families, revolved around birthdays, anniversaries and Christmas. Christmas was always celebrated at Windsor (and often still is) and, because she knew it would please Albert, Victoria had all the principal rooms decked out with Christmas trees to remind him of his native Coburg.

In May 1843, a month after the birth of Princess Alice, the whole family went to Claremont to celebrate the Queen's birthday. Albert had secretly commissioned Landseer to paint a portrait of the new addition to the family (she was number three), and the artist had been smuggled into the nursery to this end. The picture shows the baby sleeping in the old Saxon cradle in which all Victoria's children began their early life. She is buried in a froth of white lace, affectionately watched over by the Queen's favourite black terrier Dandie. Albert adored birthdays. Six hundred years earlier Edward I, too, had been partial to these occasions and every year on his son's birthday he gave a great

185

Victoria and Albert with their children around the Christmas tree at Windsor Castle

feast at Caernarvon Castle for as many poor people times one hundred as his son's age; so when little Prince Edward was six, a feast was prepared for six hundred guests. Albert's idea of birthdays was a little more intimate. For Victoria's birthday in 1843 he placed the Landseer portrait on top of a heap of other birthday gifts under a huge flower arrangement in the Claremont breakfast room. Wearing his rainbow-coloured silk dressing gown, he got up bright and early at eight and went down to the nursery to collect Vicky, who was looking ravishingly pretty in a white muslin dress embroidered with lilies of the valley. He carried his daughter back to the Queen's bedroom where they sat on the bed and wished her many happy returns, and then adjourned to the breakfast room to unwrap the presents and drool over the portrait.

The royal families of England have always loved pets. The present Queen and her corgis are inseparable, but her ancestors had wilder tastes. Edward IV as a child would sit down to meals or even go to church with his hawk on his wrist. Medieval princesses kept larks and magpies in cages, princes befriended pet monkeys, brought home from the Crusades, squirrels or fine white rats.

Medieval royal children would also have played common enough games – 'Hood man's buff', 'frog in the middle', and 'hot cockles' – and strange old-fashioned cricket with wooden, wool or leather balls, just like other ordinary children. But they probably had more toys than most: silver rattles for the little ones; painted wooden crossbows and toy horses for their older brothers and sisters.

Nearer our own time, little princesses played with doll's houses. Queen Mary's is a favourite attraction at Windsor Castle, and so too is the one presented to the little Princess Elizabeth of York by the people of Wales, which now stands in the grounds at Windsor. It has been enjoyed by all the Queen's children, and now by her grandchildren. It is just large enough for a child to stand up in – grown-ups stay outside. It has real taps, a real kettle, and curtains at every window.

Prince Albert surpassed even this for his children: he had what must be one of the first ever pre-fabricated houses shipped over from Germany and re-erected in the grounds of Osborne House on the Isle of Wight. It was a replica of a Swiss chalet, perfect in

187

Princess Elizabeth with one of her corgis, Dookie

Six of the children of Frederick, Prince of Wales and Augusta of Saxe-Gotha at play, with a dog-cart, bow and arrows, and their pets

every detail with a gabled roof, wooden shutters, and an upper-floor balcony. The children were charmed with it. Just as Marie Antoinette played at being a milkmaid at Le Hameau at Versailles, the little princes and princesses played at keeping house. The girls cleaned, cooked and entertained visitors to tea. The boys did carpentry, chopped wood and played at being soldiers in a small replica fort nearby. Albert gave them all presents of gardening tools and wheelbarrows one Christmas with their names on the handles to encourage them to take an interest in nature. It was a children's paradise to stand on the balcony of their Swiss cottage, looking out to sea with a pair of borrowed binoculars, watching all the exciting ships that came and went into Portsmouth Harbour across the Solent. It could well have been this that gave the male members of the Royal Family a taste for future naval life.

As Victoria and Albert's children grew older, and also grew in number, they arranged extravagant domestic theatricals to which their parents, other members of the family, and palace staff were invited. In 1854, to celebrate their parents' wedding anniversary,

the seven little Saxe-Coburgs staged a musical comedy called *The Four Seasons*, devised by thirteen-year-old Princess Vicky. Prince Leopold was just three months old. It was an ambitious production. Princess Alice kicked off the show as the 'Spirit of Spring', scattering flowers over the stage and reciting verses. Then came Princess Vicky with little Prince Arthur in tow (wearing little but a few strategically-placed flowers much to his mother's chagrin) singing about the joys of summer. Next came

another skimpily clad Prince, this time Alfred, clad in a panther skin and blowing a hunting horn in the name of Autumn. The last scene showed Bertie as Winter decked out with icicles, and his youngest sister Louise as a snow princess. For an epilogue Princess Helena, looking part-druid, part-vestal-virgin in white, gave a solemn blessing to her parents.

It was all very jolly; Prince Albert behind his Teutonic façade had a great sense of fun. He once built a brick castle for baby Bertie in the nursery which was so tall he had to stand on a chair to put the turret on top. He loved playing the organ in the drawing-room at Windsor with a child sitting on either knee. The Victorians loved musical evenings. and Victoria's own family was no exception. On another of the Queen's birthdays, her thirty-ninth in May 1858, there was a family concert at their favourite home of Osborne. Afterwards the Queen wrote to Vicky (who had just got married) about the recital, which followed immediately after luncheon:

1   Arthur and Alice played a little duet.

2   Louise a little piece alone, fairly but not in time.

3   Alice and Lenchen [her nickname for Princess Helena] a duet beautifully.

4   Alice and Alfie a duet on the Violin and a little composition of his own very pretty and of which he is not a little proud.

5   Alice a long beautiful and very difficult sonata by Beethoven.

Arthur recited a German poem and Lenchen and Louis have something to say which, however, has not yet been said.

Being a royal child in a loving family sounds almost too idyllic and it is a relief to know that royal children could also be rude, disobedient, and undisciplined. Gone were the days of the whipping boys, and Prince Albert believed in corporal punishment for his sons at least, while the girls when naughty were confined to their rooms. But from the earliest age Bertie, the Prince of Wales, was a thorn in his parents' flesh. He swore at his tutors, refused to do his lessons, and threw stones at those masters who dared to discipline him. A generation later the story was worse. His own children were the scourge of the neighbourhood, especially his three daughters, Louise, Victoria and Maud. It was doubtless a reaction against the severity of his own upbringing that persuaded Bertie to allow his children to rampage through their youth without chastising them. The three Wales Princesses were what their grandmother described as 'poor frail little fairies' at birth but, as luck would have it, they did not grow up to inherit their mother Princess Alexandra's good looks. They had thin mousy hair, pale protruding eyes and bad complexions, but above all they had spirit. The Duke of Devonshire once unwittingly lent the Wales family his house at Chiswick and the children tore through the ornamental gardens like Furies leaving a trail of destruction, overturned statues, broken obelisks and uprooted shrubs. When the gardener tried to intervene, they set about him kicking him in the shins. Mothers trembled when they were told that the Wales children were coming to visit and urged their own little treasures to lock up their toys or they would surely be destroyed. Once during a meal when his grandmother, the Queen, was present, the future George v behaved so badly that he

Albert Edward, Prince of Wales and Alexandra with their two sons, George, who became George V, and Albert Victor (Eddy), the Duke of Clarence

was ordered to sit under the table for the duration of lunch. When the board had been cleared he was summoned forth to apologize and horrified the company by emerging stark naked.

Part of the problem was that Bertie was rarely at home and the children were left in the care of their indulgent mother Princess Alexandra whom they always referred to as 'Darling Mother Dear'. Soon after Bertie had married Alexandra, he had gone back to his old Lothario ways, leaving his wife alone to cope with the children. During her third confinement she had contracted rheumatic fever which had left her with a slight limp and a tendency to deafness which obviously irritated Bertie. He was undoubtedly fond of his children but fonder of pursuing his own profligate ways, excusing himself by saying 'I think a child is always best looked after under its mother's eye.'

Four of the children of Prince George and Princess May, standing to attention under the watchful eye of a Highland officer. Left to right, Edward (the future Edward VIII), Albert (the future George VI) Henry, Duke of Gloucester, and Mary, the Princess Royal

Royal grandparents – like most grandparents – have tended to over-indulge. Though Victoria may have said of the Wales children 'Such ill-bred, ill-trained children! I cannot fancy them at all,' she always remembered their birthdays and had them to stay at Windsor when Bertie was dangerously ill at Sandringham. When Prince George was eight she sent him a watch as a present, saying in the accompanying note that she hoped 'that it will serve to remind you to be very punctual in every thing and ever exact in your duties.'

When the old Queen died and Bertie at last, after sixty years as Heir Apparent, became King he too was an indulgent grand-parent. The new Prince and Princess of Wales, Prince George and Princess Mary, went on an extensive tour of the British Empire including India, and Edward and Alexandra had the grand-children up from York Cottage, Sandringham, to stay at Bucking-ham Palace and shamelessly spoiled them. Edward was asked by his grandmother what he would like most in the world and he replied 'to go for a ride in a taxi please, Grandmother'. Without further ado a taxi was summoned and the pair of them went off for a spin, savouring the untold delights of thick leather upholstery and a rubber klaxon in the shape of a lightbulb.

It was as well that Edward VII and Alexandra were such devoted grandparents, for Prince George and Princess Mary were rather distant and found it hard to be demonstrative parents. George, forgetting his own mischievousness as a child, insisted that his two elder sons behave from the very first like naval officers, while a comic snapshot of his four elder children shows them being drilled in the grounds of Sandringham behind a piper, with another Highland officer shouting out their marching orders. All the children, including Princess Mary, have toy rifles over their shoulders. Their father was extremely strict. He was once so annoyed to see Edward standing with his hands thrust into his trouser pockets that he ordered the children's nanny, Mrs Bill, to sew up the pockets of all the boys' trousers. And in later life when he became Duke of Windsor, Edward remarked, 'No words that I was ever to hear could be so disconcerting to the spirit as the summons, usually delivered by a footman, "His Royal Highness wishes to see you in the Library".' It was usually little Bertie who was summoned to the library to face his father's anger for Bertie was something of a scape-goat in the family. Everything seemed to be against him – his knock knees, his stammer, and his shyness. And yet in later life he remembered his childhood as a happy one. He recalled sitting on low-cushioned stools with his brothers and sister sewing comforters for one of his mother's many charities and listening to her reading them all fairy stories.

In turn he became a devoted family man. He and the Duchess of York and the two little little Princesses, Elizabeth and Margaret Rose, would drive off for the weekend to the Royal Lodge at Windsor and everyone, chauffeur, kitchen staff, cook, would go down to the woods to undertake strenuous clearing and firewood gathering. By this time Lillibet had grown out of her childish mischievousness which as a curious three-year-old had prompted her to walk backwards and forwards in front of the guard at Buckingham Palace to see how often he would present arms, or as a schoolgirl of six, bored with the monotony of grammar, to tip an inkwell over her head.

Princess Elizabeth and the Duke of Edinburgh, sitting with their elder children, Prince Charles and Princess Anne, in the gardens at Clarence House

While I was researching this book, small but vivid vignettes about royal princes and princesses through history stayed in my mind.

Henry VIII's fourteen-year-old sister, Margaret Tudor, going off to marry James IV of Scotland with a trousseau that included six pairs of slippers and twenty-four pairs of gloves, while his other sister, Mary, went off to marry Louis XIII of France so weighed down with goldsmith's work on her mantle and crown that she could not dismount to greet and kiss her future husband.

The pretty and serious little nine-year-old Princess Elizabeth, sister of Charles I and later the Winter Queen, who, on being told that Guy Fawkes at his execution had declared that he wanted to put the princess on the throne instead of her father, had replied with the solemnity that only a nine-year-old princess could muster: 'What a Queen should I have made by this means. I had rather been blown up with my royal father in the Parliament House than wear his crown on such condition.'

196

The strange procession of Queen Charlotte and her thirteen children leaving Kew on their way to their model farm at Richmond to play at milking cows and herding sheep.

The Duchess of York's etiquette game which she played with her daughters Elizabeth and Margaret Rose to teach them how to address people:

'All right,' says the Duchess, 'Now I'm the Prime Minister.'

'Good morning, Mr Baldwin,' says Princess Elizabeth.

'And now', continues the Duchess, 'I'm the Archbishop of Canterbury.'

'Good morning, your Grace,' pipes up Margaret Rose.

And the faded memento in Buckingham Palace of a child's ration card number MAPMA/96, which was issued to Princess Anne as a post-war but still rationable baby.

The keynote of today's royal parents is their determination to keep family life sacred. It is neatly summed up by Princess Anne, who recently said: 'The greatest advantage of my entire life is the family I grew up in. The family was always there, the feeling of being in a family, and we are the stronger for it.'

Family Trees

These have been drawn up to show how the people mentioned in this book are related to each other, so they have been kept as simple as possible. Princes and princesses not referred to in the book have not been included, but their existence is indicated in the family trees.

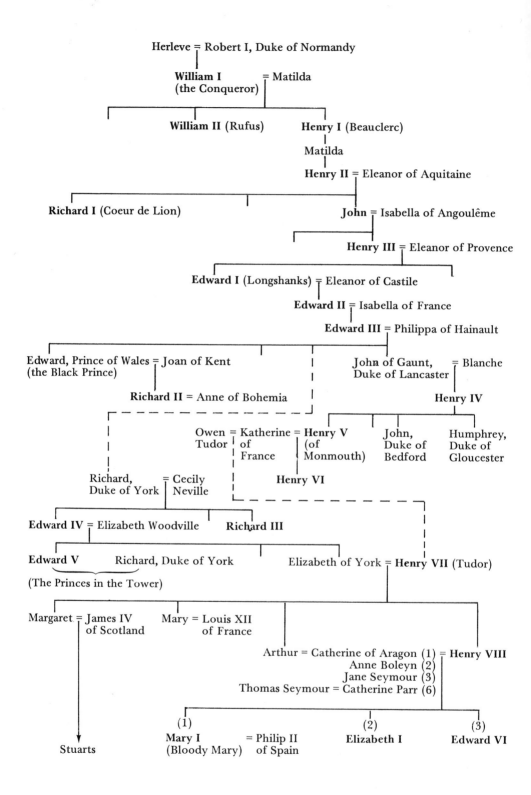

Herleve = Robert I, Duke of Normandy

William I (the Conqueror) = Matilda

William II (Rufus)   Henry I (Beauclerc)

Matilda

Henry II = Eleanor of Aquitaine

Richard I (Coeur de Lion)   John = Isabella of Angoulême

Henry III = Eleanor of Provence

Edward I (Longshanks) = Eleanor of Castile

Edward II = Isabella of France

Edward III = Philippa of Hainault

Edward, Prince of Wales = Joan of Kent (the Black Prince)   John of Gaunt, Duke of Lancaster = Blanche

Richard II = Anne of Bohemia   Henry IV

Owen Tudor = Katherine of France = Henry V (of Monmouth)   John, Duke of Bedford   Humphrey, Duke of Gloucester

Richard, Duke of York = Cecily Neville   Henry VI

Edward IV = Elizabeth Woodville   Richard III

Edward V   Richard, Duke of York   Elizabeth of York = Henry VII (Tudor)

(The Princes in the Tower)

Margaret = James IV of Scotland   Mary = Louis XII of France

Arthur = Catherine of Aragon (1) = Henry VIII
Anne Boleyn (2)
Jane Seymour (3)
Thomas Seymour = Catherine Parr (6)

(1)   (2)   (3)

Stuarts   Mary I (Bloody Mary) = Philip II of Spain   Elizabeth I   Edward VI

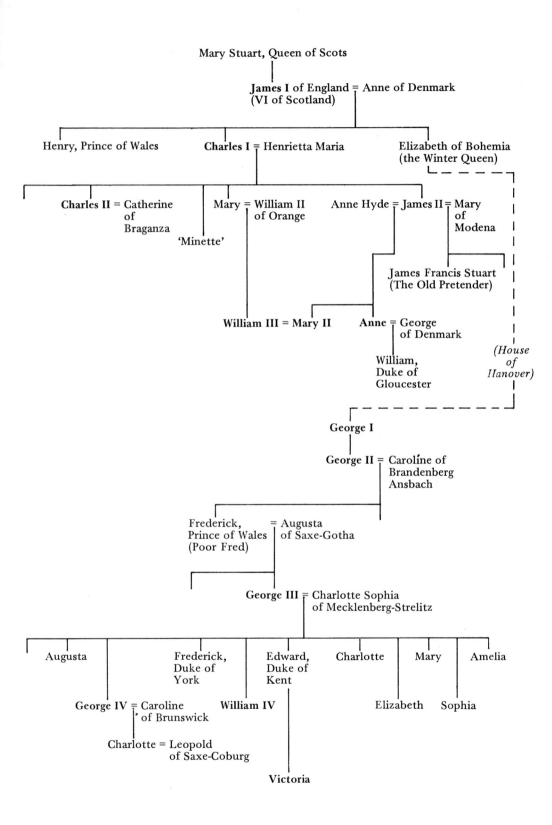

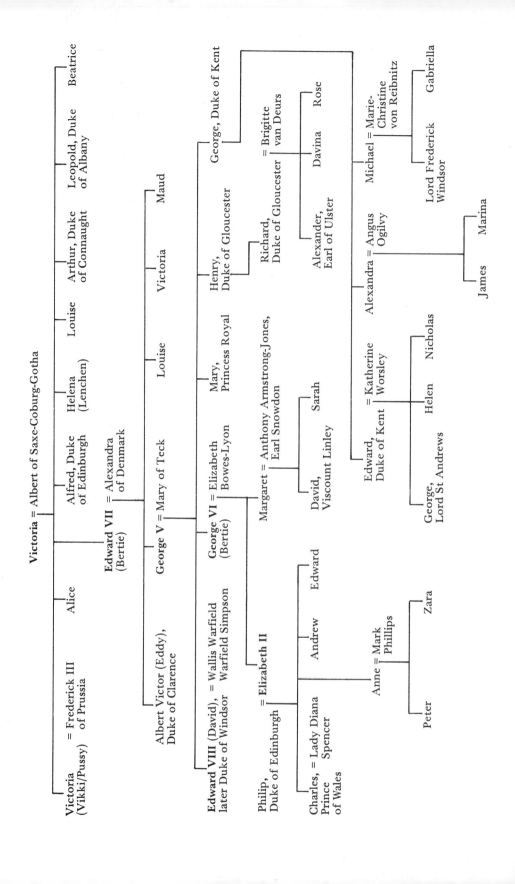

Index

207

Picture Acknowledgements

The pictures on pages 54, 58, 61, 63, 64, 77, 94, 104, 117, 128, 134-5, 146, 148, 174, 176, 182-3, 189 are reproduced by gracious permission of H.M. the Queen. Photographs and illustrations were supplied or are reproduced by kind permission of the following: British Library: 12, 102, 121, 162, 163; Camera Press: 67; Central Press: 83; John Freeman: 18, 42, 51, 53, 97; Tim Graham: 7; Keystone Press Agency: 73; Mansell Collection: 20, 23, 25, 31, 70-1, 80, 82, 88, 132, 137, 166, 168, 186, 191; National Portrait Gallery: 154; Popperfoto: 15, 35, 37, 40, 46-7, 85, 100, 101, 107, 108, 109, 131, 140, 150, 184, 188, 190, 193, 194, 196; Radio Times Hulton Picture Library: 55.

Picture research by Philippa Lewis

DATE DUE

GAYLORD · PRINTED IN U.S.A.